ANTICHRIST:

THE SEARCH FOR AMALEK

*"Because the LORD has sworn: the LORD will have
war with Amalek from generation to generation"*
—Exodus 17:16.

RC MORRO

PRESS

Antichrist: The Search for Amalek
"Because the LORD has sworn: the LORD will have war with Amalek from generation to generation" Exodus 17:16.
by RC Morro

Printed in the United States of America

ISBN 9781629526140

www.xulonpress.com

ACKNOWLEDGMENTS

To Mom, for her love of the Bible

To Dr. Brad, for leading me to Jesus Christ

To Vason, for patiently listening

To Pastor Dan, for spiritual guidance

To Debbie, for the first read

DEDICATION

To the memory of Jack Kinsella – his daily Omega Letter inspired me to write this book.

And to my wife, Lalia, whose love of the Truth and attention to detail made her the perfect editor.

CONTENTS

PREFACE

There were many mass murderers in history, including Mao of China (49–78 million), Joseph Stalin of Russia (8-20 million) and Leopold of Belgium (2-15 million). Each one is a frightening example of mankind's insanity.

There is a subtle difference between these three and, say, Adolf Hitler. Hitler directed most of his fury at one particular people—the Jews. That is a different type of hatred. It desires more than to just shed blood; it desires to wipe the slate clean of the memory of an entire race of people.

That kind of hatred is described by the Psalmist Asaph: *"Come, and let us cut them off from being a nation, that the name of Israel may be remembered no more"* (Ps. 83:4).

Christians call this type of killer Antichrist, Man of Sin, Deceiver of the Brethren, and Son of Perdition. Medieval Jewish literature calls him *Armilus* or anti-Messiah. Armilus appears frequently in the later apocalyptic Midrashim literature, declaring himself to be god and demanding worship.

The Bible gives us clues as to his origins in one of the most perplexing passages in God's word.

"And Jacob I have loved, But Esau I have hated" Malachi 3:1-2.

INTRODUCTION

Throughout recorded history, men have speculated about the identity of the final antichrist. Many names have emerged: Herod, Nero, Hitler, John F. Kennedy, and even Prince Charles of Wales.

Conjecture rages about his origins, race, and religion. Will he be an evil pope, president, or politician? Much has also been written about the timing of his appearance.

The Prophet Daniel

Daniel 9:26 says that the final antichrist will emerge from the Roman Empire, the same world power that destroyed the Jewish temple in AD 70.

In Daniel 2:31–43, the prophet interpreted King Nebuchadnezzar's dream and prophesied a statue that represented four kingdoms that would rule Israel and most of the world with great power.

The first kingdom, represented by the head of gold, was Babylon ruled by Nebuchadnezzar.

The second kingdom was Medo-Persia, represented by the silver chest and arms.

The third empire was Greece under Alexander, represented by the brass belly and thighs.

The fourth empire was Rome and Constantinople, represented by the two legs of iron. This fourth empire will be revived in the last days and will be a confederation of ten kingdoms depicted by the ten toes of the statue (Dan. 7:24).

Daniel said the feet and toes were made of iron and clay, meaning that the empire will be partially strong and partially weak, an accurate description of the EU (twenty-eight nations) today.

In Daniel 9:27, the prophet says, *"Then he shall confirm a covenant [peace treaty] with many for one week."* That false seven-year peace marks the beginning of the seven-year tribulation period.

Using the Bible's guardrails, expect the EU to continue to grow (seventy nations) until its footprint is the same as the ancient Roman Empire.

The Jewish Feast of Purim

Three years ago, I was working on a post about the Jewish feast of Purim for my blog. I was particularly fascinated by the evil anti-Semite, Haman, in the book of Esther. A few months later, I began a paper trying to ascertain if Haman could be a link in an evil bloodline of murderers of Jews throughout history. I was looking for a connection.

To discover the origin of this bloodline, I went to the best source to find beginnings, the book of Genesis. The first book of the Bible provided several clues about a divergent line in the story about Isaac and Rebekah's twin boys.

Genesis 25:23

Beginning with Esau as the root of the hatred of the Jewish bloodline, the most heinous eradicators of Jews throughout history can be found. That kinship and spirit will ultimately lead to the final Man of Sin, Antichrist.

In one of the most amazing stories in the Bible, the pregnant Rebekah asked God about the turmoil inside her. Genesis 25:23 says, *"And the Lord said to her 'Two nations are in your womb, two peoples shall be separated from your body; one people shall be stronger than the other, and the older shall serve the younger."*

Two nations emerged, Arab (Esau) and Jew (Jacob). The two nations have been at enmity with each other ever since. In Genesis 25:22, we learn that the twins, Jacob and Esau, fought in the womb. And, in verse 24, *"So when her days were fulfilled for her to give birth, indeed there were twins in her womb. And the first came out red. He was like a hairy garment all over; so they called his name Esau."*

It took four thousand years for science to catch up with the word of God. On December 3, 2012 ABC News published an ultrasound video showing proof that twins do indeed fight in the womb, even pointing out that one twin can dominate the blood supply of the other by what is termed the twin-to-twin transfusion syndrome.

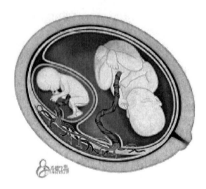

Twin-Twin Transfusion Syndrome.
Reproduced by permission from St. Louis
Fetal Care Institute, St. Louis, MO

"The condition causes the twins' blood flow to essentially become interconnected. One baby inevitably loses out to the other, receiving less blood, and stops growing. The other baby then grows dangerously fast, putting it at risk of cardio-vascular complications."[1]

The Bible's comment that Esau was a very red baby indicates that the twin-to-twin transfusion syndrome had occurred and Esau was the larger baby.

Questions That Beg for an Answer

I wanted to understand why Malachi 1:2-3 and Romans 9:13 state that God loved Jacob and hated Esau. I couldn't find any other reference to God hating anyone by name, and I was curious as to why He hated Esau, and not Ishmael.

I wondered why Esau's descendants, the Edomites, were determined to kill people of their own bloodline, and why God said in Exodus 17:16 that He would have war with Esau's grandson Amalek in every generation.

I wanted to know if there was any connection between Esau's descendants and the Jews who chose Barabbas over Jesus. Also, why did Jesus call the scribes and Pharisees a brood of vipers?

And lastly, why would one of Jesus' disciples, after spending three years with Him, betray Him for thirty pieces of silver?

In the chapters that follow, I will attempt to show the movement of Esau's bloodline from Israel to Jordan, back to Israel, and from there throughout the world.

That same bloodline exhibits a murderous hatred of the Jews throughout history.

CHAPTER 1

ESAU: ANTICHRIST #1, THE ROOT

The Covenant: 4,000 BC

When Abram was ninety-nine years old, the LORD appeared to Abram and said to him, "I am Almighty God; walk before Me and be blameless. And I will make My covenant between Me and you, and will multiply you exceedingly." Then Abram fell on his face, and God talked with him, saying: "As for Me, behold, My covenant is with you, and you shall be a father of many nations. No longer shall your name be called Abram, but your name shall be Abraham; for I have made you a father of many nations. I will make you exceedingly fruitful; and I will make nations of you, and kings shall come from you. And I will establish My covenant between Me and you and your descendants after you in their generations, for an everlasting covenant, to be God to you and your descendants after you. Also I give to you and your descendants after you the land in which you are a stranger, all the land of Canaan, as an everlasting possession; and I will be their God."

And God said to Abraham: "As for you, you shall keep My covenant, you and your descendants after you throughout their generations. This is My covenant which you shall keep, between Me and you and your descendants after you: Every male child among you shall be circumcised; and you shall be circumcised in the flesh of your foreskins, and it shall be a sign of the covenant between Me and you. He who is eight days old among you shall be circumcised, every male child in your generations, he who is born in your house or bought with money from any foreigner who is not your descendant. He who is born in your house and he who is bought with your money must be circumcised, and My covenant shall be in your flesh for an everlasting covenant. *And the uncircumcised male child, who is not circumcised in the flesh of his foreskin, that person shall be cut off from his people; he has broken My covenant.*"

—Genesis 17:1–14, emphasis added

Ishmael

Now God had promised Abraham and Sarah a son. Sarah, thinking that she was too old to bear a child, prompted Abraham to sleep with her handmaiden to help God's promise come to pass. Ishmael, Abraham's son with the Egyptian handmaiden Hagar, was thirteen years old when Abraham circumcised him. Abraham obeyed God and circumcised his whole household on that very day, and *"because Ishmael kept the covenant, God promised to make him a great nation"* (Gen. 21:18).

The Birth of Isaac

God was gracious to Abraham and Sarah despite their interference, and their promised son was eventually born. Sarah had been told by God to name the child *Isaac*, which means "laughter," since Sarah had laughed to herself when she overheard God tell Abraham that she would bear a son in her old age. Abraham circumcised Isaac on the eighth day, and a great feast was held.

Rabbi Louis Ginzberg taught at the Jewish Theological Seminary for over fifty years (1903–1953) and specialized in Talmudic/Midrash studies.

In his signature work, *The Legend of the Jews*, volume 1, Rabbi Ginzberg wrote:

When Isaac grew up, quarrels broke out between him and Ishmael, on account of the rights of the first-born. Ishmael insisted he should receive a double portion of the inheritance after the death of Abraham, and Isaac should receive only one portion.

Ishmael, who had been accustomed from his youth to use the bow and arrow, was in the habit of aiming his missiles in the direction of Isaac, saying at the same time that he was but jesting. Sarah, however, insisted that Abraham make-over to Isaac all he owned, that no disputes might arise after his death.

Furthermore, Sarah insisted that Abraham divorce himself from Hagar, the mother of Ishmael, and send away the woman and her son so that there be naught in common between them and her own son, either in this world or in the future world.

Of all the trials Abraham had to undergo, none was so hard to bear as this, for it grieved him sorely to separate himself from his son. God appeared to him in the following night, and said to him: "Abraham, knowest thou not that Sarah was appointed to be thy wife from her mother's womb? She is thy companion and the wife of thy youth, and I named not Hagar as thy wife, nor Sarah as thy bondwoman."[2]

God told Abraham to listen to Sarah because it was through Isaac that God's promises would be fulfilled. God also promised him that Ishmael would be blessed and a great nation would come from him, despite God's warning that *"he shall be a wild man; his hand shall be against every man, and every man's hand against him. And he shall dwell in the presence of all his brethren"* (Gen. 16:12).

Those same seeds of resentment are apparent in the descendants of Ishmael towards the descendants of Isaac today. Islam claims its roots in Ishmael, as he was the eldest son of Abraham and the ancestor of the prophet Muhammad. Islam teaches that it was Ishmael who was to be sacrificed on Mount Moriah, not Isaac. Ishmael was sent east of the family to the Arabian Peninsula, which today is Saudi Arabia.

Isaac Marries Rebekah

When it came time for Isaac to marry, Abraham sent his trusted servant to find a wife from his family's home in Nahor so that Isaac would not marry a Canaanite woman but marry in the family line. As the servant reached Nahor, he bowed to worship God.

> Then he said, "O LORD God of my master Abraham, please give me success this day, and show kindness to my master Abraham. Behold, here I stand by the well of water, and the daughters of the men of the city are coming out to draw water. Now let it be that the young woman to whom I say, 'Please let down your pitcher that I may drink,' and she says, 'Drink, and I will also give your camels a drink'—let her be the one You have appointed for Your servant Isaac. And by this I will know that You have shown kindness to my master."

—Genesis 24:12–14

Before the servant finished praying, Rebekah came out and fulfilled every word that the servant had prayed and then brought him to her family, where the servant gave gifts that he had brought from Abraham.

With the permission of her brother Laban, Rebekah agreed to journey with the servant to meet her future husband.

> Now Isaac came from the way of Beer Lahai Roi, for he dwelt in the South. And Isaac went out to meditate in the field in the evening; and he lifted his eyes and looked, and there, the camels were coming. Then Rebekah lifted her eyes, and when she saw Isaac she dismounted from her camel; for she had said to the servant, "Who is this man walking in the field to meet us?"

> The servant said, "It is my master." So she took a veil and covered herself.

> And the servant told Isaac all the things that he had done. Then Isaac brought her into his mother Sarah's tent; and he took Rebekah and she became his wife, and he loved her. So Isaac was comforted after his mother's death.

> —Genesis 24:62–67

Is Isaac and Rebekah's Wedding a Foreshadowing of the Rapture?

In the ancient Jewish wedding, tradition held that the father of the groom would select the bride for his son. In a beautiful illustration of foreshadowing, the father represents God, the son represents Jesus, the servant is the Holy Spirit, and the bride represents the church. The Jewish wedding feast could only begin when the father (God) told his son (Jesus) to go and get his bride (church rapture).

In Matthew 25:1–13, the parable of the five wise (ready) and five foolish (not ready) virgins may provide a clue as to the number of Christians that will be taken to meet Christ in the air. The parable teaches that when the groom (Son) was directed by the father (God) to get his bride (church), only five (half) of the ten virgins were ready. *"Afterward the other virgins came also, saying, 'Lord, Lord, open to us!' But he answered and said, 'Assuredly, I say to you, I do not know you. Watch therefore, for you know neither the day nor the hour in which the Son of Man is coming"* (vv. 11–13).

If we apply this parable to the end of the church age, the number of Christians taken will be half, or 1 billion, of the approximately 2.1 billion that call themselves Christians today.

Twins: Two Nations Are in Your Womb

Isaac prayed to the Lord for his wife because she was barren. Rebekah became pregnant, but the babies struggled within her, and she prayed to the Lord to know what was wrong.

And the Lord said to her: "Two nations are in your womb, two peoples shall be separated from your body; one people shall be stronger than the other, and the older shall serve the younger."

So when her days were fulfilled for her to give birth, indeed there were twins in her womb. And the first came out red. He was like a hairy garment all over; so they called his name Esau. Afterward his brother came out, and his hand took hold of Esau's heel; so his name was called Jacob. Isaac was sixty years old when she bore them.

—Genesis 25:23–26

Rabbi Ginzberg says, "The quarrel between the two brothers regarding the birthright had its beginning before they emerged from the womb of their mother. Each desired to be the first to come into the world. It was only when Esau threatened to carry his point at the expense of his mother's life that Jacob gave way."[3]

In her book, *The Esau Effect*, author Kimberly Rogers writes that "Esau was kicking Jacob's head in an attempt to kill him. Esau's kicking heel would have CRUSHED Jacob's head if Jacob had not reached up to stop it. Jacob was not trying to usurp Esau. Esau was trying to be the only baby born."[4]

"So the boys grew. And Esau was a skillful hunter, a man of the field; but Jacob was a mild man, dwelling in tents. And Isaac

loved Esau because he ate of his game, but Rebekah loved Jacob" (Gen. 25:27–28).

Esau Sells His Birthright

> Now Jacob cooked a stew; and Esau came in from the field, and he was weary. And Esau said to Jacob, "Please feed me with that same red stew, for I am weary." Therefore his name was called Edom.
>
> But Jacob said, "Sell me your birthright as of this day."
>
> And Esau said, "Look, I am about to die; so what is this birthright to me?"
>
> Then Jacob said, "Swear to me as of this day."
>
> So he swore to him, and sold his birthright to Jacob. And Jacob gave Esau bread and stew of red lentils; then he ate and drank, arose, and went his way. Thus Esau despised his birthright.
>
> —Genesis 25:29–34

Esau sold his birthright to Jacob for 'red' pottage, therefore his name was called EDOM, meaning red.

Did Esau Break Covenant?

Although the Bible is silent regarding Jacob's and Esau's circumcisions, we can draw upon the extra-Biblical work of rabbis in the oral Torah, which was passed down through the ages with astounding precision. It is reasonable to assume that the ancient Jewish teachings found in the oral Torah were given accuracy by God's guidance through the generations in order to preserve the genealogies and the division of the Promised Land.

Rabbi Ginzberg writes:

> The circumstances connected with the birth of her twin sons were as remarkable as those during the period of Rebekah's pregnancy. Esau was the first to see the light, and with him all impurity came from the womb; Jacob was born clean and sweet of body. Esau was brought forth with hair, beard, and teeth, both front and back, and he was blood-red, a sign of his future sanguinary nature.
>
> On account of his ruddy appearance he [Esau] remained uncircumcised. Isaac, his father, feared that it [his ruddy appearance] was due to poor circulation of the blood, and he hesitated to perform the circumcision. He decided to wait until Esau should attain his thirteenth year, the age at which Ishmael had received the sign of the covenant. But when Esau grew up, he refused to give heed to his father's wish, and so he was left uncircumcised. The opposite of his brother in this

as in all respects, Jacob was born with the sign of the covenant upon his body, a rare distinction. But Esau also bore a mark upon him at birth, the figure of a serpent, the symbol of all that is wicked and hated of God.[5]

What Is the Sign of Covenant?

Being born under the sign of covenant is called *aposthia*, which the medical dictionary defines as to be born without a prepuce, or foreskin.

To be born circumcised was regarded as the privilege of the saints, from Adam, "who was made in the image of God," and Moses to Zerubbabel... Uncircumcision, being considered a blemish, circumcision was to remove it and to render Abraham and his descendants 'perfect'.[6]

Extra-Biblical sources tell us that Jacob and his son Joseph were also born aposthic.[7]

Jewish law required males born without a foreskin, or who lost their foreskin through means other than a formal circumcision ceremony, to have a drop of blood let from their penis at the point where the foreskin would have been (or was) attached. The *blood of the covenant* must be drawn from the glans.[8]

The Figure of the Serpent

Esau bore a mark of the figure of a serpent, but the Talmud gives no further description of it.

There are three marks noted in the Bible, one in Genesis and two in Revelation, with which Bible scholars have struggled and God has chosen not to reveal:

- The mark that protected Cain from being killed: *"And the LORD set a mark on Cain, lest anyone finding him should kill him"* (Gen. 4:15).

- The future mark that will protect the 144,000 Jewish male virgins: *"And I heard the number of those who were sealed. One hundred and forty-four thousand of all the tribes of the children of Israel were sealed [on their foreheads]"* (Rev. 7:4).

- The future mark of the beast: *"He causes all, both small and great, rich and poor, free and slave, to receive a mark on their right hand or on their foreheads, and that no one may buy or sell except one who has the mark or the name of the beast, or the number of his name"* (Rev. 13:16–17).

God Intended the Birthright for Jacob

The twins were very different. Esau, a hunter, was strong and fierce with a sword. He was favored by his father, Isaac. Jacob is described in the Bible as a tent dweller, a gentle man, patient and kind to his mother Rebekah, who favored him.

Rebekah was afraid that Isaac might not obey the oracle of God in which He gave preference to the younger. She decided to intervene. She disguised Jacob as Esau and presented him for blessing to Isaac, who was blind and dying. Later, when Esau came for his blessing and found out that it had already been given to Jacob, he became furious and asked Isaac for another.

Here is an important point to remember: God had promised *before* their births that the elder son would serve the younger (Gen. 25:23) and that the blessings normally reserved for the elder would go to the younger. God clearly decreed that the birthright was intended for Jacob. Yet many people assume that through trickery and deception, Jacob stole it from Esau.

Sound familiar? This four-thousand-year-old conflict is similar to the Israeli (Jacob) and Arab-Palestinian (Esau) conflict of today. When the Ottoman Empire collapsed at the end of World War I in 1919, the land of Palestine was divided by the League of Nations. In 1922, the League awarded the area of Palestine, Transjordan, and Iraq to Britain. The League awarded mandates over Syria and Lebanon to France.

The Arab refugees remaining in Palestine after the war were denied citizenship in every Arab nation except Jordan, where they were allowed limited citizenship.[9] Thousands were stuck in the Promised Land with nowhere to go.

These Arab peoples were eventually offered a state beside the Jewish state in 1947, but they refused it and chose war instead. Today most nations of the world consider the Jewish state stolen and the Jews as occupiers.

That these two peoples who came from Rebekah's womb would be in perpetual conflict can be found in Genesis 27:41: *"Esau held a grudge against Jacob because of the blessing his father had given him. He said to himself, 'The days of mourning for my father are near; then I will kill my brother Jacob.' "*

Esau is still trying to kill his brother Jacob.

Two Blessings, Two Outcomes

To Jacob: *"May God give you heaven's dew and earth's rich-ness—an abundance of grain and new wine. May nations serve* *you and peoples bow down to you. Be lord over your brothers, and may the sons of your mother bow down to you. May those who curse you be cursed and those who bless you be blessed"* (Gen. 27:28–29 NIV).

Here is the prophecy inside the blessing: Jacob (Israel) was promised the fatness of the earth and that the nations would bow down to him. Never in history have the nations bowed to Israel, but in the millennial reign of Jesus Christ, the nation of Israel will be His dwelling place. All Jews will dwell there and so, the regathering of the Jews will be complete.

Jerusalem will be where He will have His sanctuary (temple) in their midst forevermore (Ezek. 37:7–11). The nations will make yearly pilgrimages to Israel to see the Lord and Jacob's blessing will be fulfilled.

To Esau: *"Your dwelling will be away from the earth's richness, away from the dew of heaven above. You will live by the sword and you will serve your brother. But when you grow restless, you will throw his yoke from off your neck"* (Gen. 27:39–40 NIV).

In Esau's blessing, the earth was given as a dwelling, not as an owner, an occupier who never feels at peace and to whom no one will ever bow down. Here is a perfect description of the Arab-Palestinians of today, as they are offered limited citizenship only in Jordan and in no other nation in the Middle East.

Jacob became the forefather of the Jews, and Esau became the forefather of the Arabs of the West Bank and Jordan. Interestingly, only Israel has offered, with conditions, citizenship in a new state within Israel. These Arab peoples were renamed "Palestinians" after World War II by Yasser Arafat.

Islam began in AD 600 and claims its heritage in Ishmael. Esau gets no mention in the Koran and is not claimed in any culture or religion.

Esau Marries Out

It is not surprising that the rebellious Esau married outside the Abrahamic bloodline. Disdaining his birthright and breaking the covenant of circumcision clearly set him as an enemy of God.

At the age of forty, Esau married Judith, the daughter of Beeri the Hittite, and Basemath, the daughter of Elon the Hittite. *"And they were a grief of mind to Isaac and Rebekah"* (Gen. 26:35).

But it was Esau's third wife, Mahalath, a daughter of Ishmael, who must have hurt Isaac the most, as it was revenge toward his father over the birthright. Like Rebekah, these pagan women came from families that worshiped idols. Rebekah, however, gave herself to the one God upon marrying Isaac. Esau's wives continued to offer incense to idols, despite living in Isaac and Rebekah's home.

Esau Must be Searched Out

We are told in Obadiah 1:6 that Esau will be searched out. Esau's deceptive cunning is hidden, while Jacob is easy to identify. Politically, the spirit of Esau (antichrist) comes in peacefully, but once in power, his evil intentions become obvious, and removing him from power is impossible short of war.

"Because of the violence against your brother Jacob, you will be covered with shame; you will be destroyed forever" (Obad.

1:10). Ironically, the Hebrew word for "violence" is *chamas*, pronounced hamas.

An example of the antichrist's spirit of deceptiveness took place in the early career of Adolf Hitler. In 1935, Winston Churchill wrote an assessment of the new German leader, Adolf Hitler:

"He might yet go down in history as the man who restored honour and peace of mind to the great Germanic nation and brought it back serene, helpful and strong, to the forefront of theEuropean family circle."[10]

It wasn't until 1941, the beginning of World War II, that the great statesman changed, and the spirit of antichrist in Hitler emerged for all to see.

Two Arab Bloodlines

All Arabs have Jewish roots through Abraham by:

- Ishmael, illegitimate son of Abraham and Sarah's Egyptian servant Hagar
- Esau, Isaac's son, who married outside the family line

Therefore, Arabs have a mixture of Jewish and Gentile blood. Malachi 1:1–3, later repeated by the apostle Paul in Romans 9:13, speaks about these twins in what could easily be one of the more controversial verses in the Bible: *"Yet Jacob I have loved, but Esau I have hated."* According to *Strong's Concordance*, the Hebrew word for *hate* that is used here means to be an enemy, an adversary, a foe; and according to the Greek translation, *hate* means to be hated; detestable.

What did God see in Jacob and Esau to say these words that seem so inequitable to us? Scholars have argued these passages for centuries. Here are three explanations for each:

Jacob I have loved . . .

1. Jacob was born circumcised, thereby keeping covenant with God.[11]
2. Jacob married according to his father's wishes in the family line (Gen. 28:6–7; 29:28).
3. Through Jacob's lineage, the Redeemer, Christ, would come (Isa. 59:20).

Esau I have hated . . .

1. Esau sold his birthright (Gen. 25:29-34) and refused circumcision, thereby breaking covenant. [12]
2. Esau married idol-worshiping women, diluting Abraham's bloodline (Gen. 36:2–12).
3. God foreknew the spirit of antichrist in Esau and refused and rejected Esau (Isa. 34:5; Jer. 49:13; Mal. 1:1–4).

Hebrews 12:14–17 NIV affirms Malachi and Romans:

Make every effort to live in peace with everyone and to be holy; without holiness no one will see the Lord. See to it that no one falls short of the grace of God and that no bitter root grows up to cause trouble and defile many. See that no one is sexually immoral, or is **godless like Esau**, who for a single meal sold his inheritance rights as the oldest son. Afterward, as you know, when he wanted to inherit this blessing, he was rejected. Even though he sought the blessing with tears, he could not change what he had done. (Emphasis added)

The hate between the two bloodlines of Jacob's and Esau's descendants has played out in bitter conflicts for over four thousand years. The enmity will continue until the final Amalek, indwelt by Satan, makes his appearance on the world stage.

Esau Moves from his Brother

In Gen. 36:6-8 Moses gives us the story of the parting of the two brothers:

Then Esau took his wives, his sons, his daughters, and all his goods which he had gained in the land of Canaan, and went to a country away from the presence of his brother Jacob. For their possessions were too great for them to dwell together and the land where they were strangers could not support them because of their livestock. So Esau dwelt in Mount Seir. Esau is Edom.

Esau was a covenant breaker. Even though the LORD allowed him to prosper in the red mountains of Edom, judgment was coming.

Son of man, set your face against Mount Seir and prophesy against it, and say to it, 'Thus says the Lord God: "Behold, O Mount Seir, I am against you; I will stretch out My hand against you, And make you most desolate; I shall lay your cities waste, And you shall be desolate. Then you shall know that I am the Lord.

Because you have had an ancient hatred, and have shed the blood of the children of Israel by the power of the sword at the time of their calamity, when their iniquity came to an end, therefore, as I live," says the Lord God, "I will prepare you for blood, and blood shall pursue you; since you have not hated blood, therefore blood shall pursue you. Thus I will make Mount Seir most desolate, and cut off from it the one who leaves and the one who returns. And I will fill its mountains with the slain; on your hills and in your valleys and in all your ravines those who are slain by the sword shall fall. I will make you perpetually desolate, and your cities shall be uninhabited; then you shall know that I am the Lord."

—Ezekiel 35:1-9

CHAPTER 2

EXODUS

It was at night when Pharaoh summoned Moses: *"Rise, go out from among my people, both you and the children of Israel. And go; serve the LORD as you have said. Also, take your flocks and your herds, as you have said, and be gone; and bless me also"* (Ex. 12:29–32).

Pharaoh had enough of the ten plagues, especially the last one that took the firstborn of the land of Egypt, including his own son. Even though the Jews were useful for labor and jobs that the average Egyptian felt was beneath him, Pharaoh was ready to let those irritating Jews go.

And go they did. There was not even enough time to let the bread rise. They were going to the Promised Land after four hundred years, led by a reluctant leader named Moses.

A year earlier, God had appeared to Moses in a burning bush and told him He was sending him to bring the Jews out of bondage in Egypt. Moses had tried to get God to assign someone else: *"Who am I that I should go to Pharaoh, and that I should bring the children of Israel out of Egypt?"* (Ex. 3:11).

But God, being God, had already decided: *"I will certainly be with you. And this shall be a sign to you that I have sent you: When you have brought the people out of Egypt, you shall serve God on this mountain"* (Ex. 3:12).

Moses, wondering how in the world he would convince these people that he had instructions from God Himself, asked, *"Indeed, when I come to the children of Israel and say to them, 'The God of your fathers has sent me to you,' and they say to me, 'What is His name?' What shall I say to them?"* (Ex. 3:13).

"God replied to Moses, 'I AM WHO I AM.' And He said, 'Thus you shall say to the children of Israel: "I AM has sent me to you."' Moreover God said to Moses, 'Thus you shall say to the children of Israel: "The LORD God of your fathers, the God of Abraham, the God of Isaac, and the God of Jacob, has sent me to you" (Ex. 3:14–15).

God chose Moses and Moses obeyed God, and the journey began. Yet even with the Lord leading, there was trouble in the exodus.

Pharaoh Changes His Mind

Now the LORD spoke to Moses, saying: "Speak to the children of Israel, that they turn and camp before Pi Hahiroth, between Migdol and the sea, opposite Baal Zephon; you shall camp before it by the sea. For Pharaoh will say of the children of Israel, 'They are bewildered by the land; the wilderness has closed them in.' Then I will harden Pharaoh's heart, so that he will pursue them; and I will gain honor over Pharaoh and over all his army, that the Egyptians may know that I am the LORD." And they did so.

—Exodus 14:1–4

After the Jews' hasty departure, things were worse, not better, in Egypt. The people complained about the work not getting done. Over one million slaves were gone, and Pharaoh was having a bad case of remorse. He remembered how Moses had demanded, "Let my people go" over and over again, followed by all kinds of calamities.

There had been ten plagues in all: water turned into blood, frogs, gnats and lice, flies, diseased livestock, boils, thunder and hail, locusts, darkness, and death of the firstborn of both man and beast.

What else could he do but get rid of those people? But now Pharaoh realized that there was no substitute for his labor force; he had to bring the Jews back. He had no choice.

"Pharaoh said to the people, 'Why have we done this that we have let Israel go from serving us?' So he made ready his chariot and took his people with him. Also, he took six hundred choice chariots, and all the chariots of Egypt with captains over every one of them" (Ex. 14:5–7).

God was going to use this situation, much like all others, to show His glory and teach the people that kings and pharaohs are nothing compared to Him.

The Red Sea Parts

The Israelites were approaching the Red Sea when they saw the Egyptian army with hundreds of chariots drawing near from behind. They bemoaned to Moses, *"Because there were no graves in Egypt, have you taken us away to die in the wilderness?"* (Ex. 14:11).

Can you just picture Moses? He hadn't really wanted this assignment to begin with. Was he tempted to throw up his hands in disgust and let these incredibly ungrateful people have a piece of his mind? That's not what happened.

The next words from Moses became the banner for many conflicts and wars that the Israelites would face over the next 3,400 years.

> And Moses said to the people, 'Do not be afraid. Stand still, and see the salvation of the LORD, which He will accomplish for you today. For the Egyptians whom you see today, you shall see again no more forever. The LORD will fight for you, and you shall hold your peace'.
>
> —Exodus 14:13–14

God Rescues His People

> Then the LORD said to Moses, "Stretch out your hand over the sea that the waters may come back upon the Egyptians, on their chariots, and on their horsemen." And Moses stretched out his hand over the sea; and when the morning appeared, the sea returned to its full depth, while the Egyptians were fleeing into it.

So the LORD overthrew the Egyptians in the midst of the sea. Then the waters returned and covered the chariots, the horsemen, and all the army of Pharaoh that came into the sea after them. Not so much as one of them remained. But the children of Israel had walked on dry land in the midst of the sea, and the waters were a wall to them on their right hand and on their left.

So the LORD saved Israel that day out of the hand of the Egyptians, and Israel saw the Egyptians dead on the seashore. Thus Israel saw the great work which the LORD had done in Egypt; so the people feared the LORD, and believed the LORD and His servant Moses.

—Exodus 14:26–31

That's it! That's how the children of God should fight the enemy: stand still in faith. The Bible is packed with examples of God and His angels fighting wars for His children. Virtually all of Israel's wars, even when they were outnumbered 500 to 1, were won miraculously through the Lord's intervention.

Jack Kinsella, in his Omega Letter website, recounts that in the wars from Israel's 1948 rebirth until recently, the Israelis were often outnumbered many times over. Reports of angels on the battlefield became common.

"During the (1973) Yom Kippur war, a lone Israeli soldier led a captured Egyptian column of tanks back to Israeli lines. When the Egyptian captain was asked why he surrendered an entire tank column back to a lone Israeli soldier, the Egyptian soldier replied, 'One soldier? There were thousands of them.' "[13]

Tension in the region among the Saudis, Jordanians, Egyptians, and Israelis has resulted in restricted availability in excavation of the sea floor. Nevertheless, these limited excavations have been able to find ancient chariot wheels at the bottom of the Red Sea.[14]

The Bible identifies the archangel Michael as Israel's guardian (Dan. 10:13, 21). The prophet Zechariah said in 12:8, *"In that day the* LORD *will defend the inhabitants of Jerusalem; the one who is feeble among them in that day shall be like David, and the house of David shall be like God, like the Angel of the* LORD *before them."*

That's why the apostle James could boldly say, *"My brethren, count it all joy when you fall into various trials"* (James 1:2), because through our trials and difficulties, we get to see the miracle of God working in our lives. But first, we must stand still in faith.

Chapter 3

AMALEK: ANTICHRIST #2

After the Red Sea crossing and the drowning of the Egyptian army, the next attack on the Israelites came from a tribe called the Amalekites. Their leader was an illegitimate grandson of Esau named Amalek, who inherited his grandfather's intense hatred (Gen. 27:41) for his brother Jacob. While the Egyptians failed to harm the Israelites, the Amalekites succeeded in doing so.

This enemy of Israel bore the name *Amalek* (Hebrew *'am*, people or nation; and *laqaq*, to lap or lick) to denote the rapidity with which he moved against Israel, for like a swarm of locusts, he flew upon them; the name furthermore designated the purpose of this enemy, who came to lick the blood of Israel.

Amalek was the son of Eliphaz and the concubine Timna, a Horite (Gen. 36:12; 1 Chron. 1:36). Esau's grandson became the chief of the Edomite tribe (Gen. 36:16) and carried on where his grandfather left off.

Once every year, on Shabbat Zachor, the Shabbat (day of rest) before Purim, every Jew is commanded to hear this passage in

Deuteronomy 25:17–18 NIV: *"Remember what the Amalekites did to you along the way when you came out of Egypt. When you were weary and worn out, they met you on your journey and attacked all who were lagging behind; they had no fear of God."*

From Ginzberg's *Legend of the Jews*:

"No sooner had he heard of Israel's departure from Egypt, than he set out against them and met them by the Red Sea. Amalek now marched from his settlement in Seir [Jordan] which was no less than four hundred parasangs [approximately 900 miles] away from the encampment of the Jews; and although five nations, the Hittites, the Hivites, the Jebusites, the Amorites, and the Canaanites, had their dwellings between his home and the camp of the Jews, he insisted upon being the first to declare war upon Israel."[15]

Amalek was twice designated in the Pentateuch (Ex. 17:14–16; Deut. 25:19) as the one against whom war should be waged until his memory be blotted out forever and became, in rabbinical literature, the type of Israel's archenemy.

Rabbi Ginzberg continues:

God punished Israel, who had shown themselves an ungrateful people, by sending against them an enemy that was ungrateful too, never recalling that he owed his life to the sons of Jacob, who had had him in their power after their brilliant victory over Esau and his followers.

In his expedition against Israel he made use of his kinsman. Before going over to open attack, he lured many unsuspecting Jews to death by his kindly words. He had fetched from Egypt the table of descent of the Jews; for every Jew had there to mark his name on the bricks produced by him.

Familiar with the names of the different Jewish families, Amalek appeared before the Jewish camp, and calling the people by name, he invited them to leave the camp, and come out to him. "Reuben! Simeon! Levi! etc.," he would call, "come out to me, your brother, and transact business with me."

Those who answered the enticing call found certain death at his hands; and not only did Amalek kill them, but he also mutilated their corpses, following the example of his grandsire Esau, by cutting off a certain part of the body, and throwing it toward heaven with the mocking words, "Here shalt Thou have what Thou desirest." In this way did he jeer at the token of the Abrahamic Covenant.

So long as the Jews remained within the encampment, he could, of course, do them no harm, for the cloud enveloped them, and under its shelter they were as well fortified as a city that is surrounded by a solid wall. The cloud, however, covered those only who were pure, but the unclean had to stay beyond it, until they were cleansed by a ritual bath, and these Amalek caught and killed. The sinners, too, particularly the tribe of Dan, who were all worshippers of idols, were not protected by the cloud, and therefore exposed to the attacks of Amalek.

Moses did not himself set out to battle against this dangerous foe of Israel, but he sent his servant Joshua, and for good reasons. Moses knew that only a descendant of Rachel, like the Ephraimite Joshua, could conquer the descendant of Esau.[15]

1400 BC: Amalekite King Wages War at Rephidim

In Exodus 17:8–15, Moses recorded a battle between the Israelites and Amalekites:

Now Amalek came and fought with Israel in Rephidim. So Moses said to Joshua, "Choose for us men, and go out and fight with Amalek. Tomorrow I will stand on the top of the hill with the staff of God in my hand." So Joshua did as Moses told him, and fought with Amalek, while Moses, Aaron, and Hur went up to the top of the hill.

Whenever Moses held up his hand, Israel prevailed, and whenever he lowered his hand, Amalek prevailed. But Moses' hands grew weary, so they took a stone and put it under him, and he sat on it, while Aaron and Hur held up his hands, one on one side, and the other on the other side. So his hands were steady until the going down of the sun.

And Joshua overwhelmed Amalek and his people with the sword. Then the LORD said to Moses, "Write this as a memorial in a book and recite it in the ears of Joshua that I will utterly blot out the memory of Amalek from under heaven." And Moses built an altar and called the name of it, The LORD is my banner, saying, 'A hand upon the throne of the Lord Jacob!'

Balaam Prophesies Against Amalek

When the Israelites camped near the kingdom of Moab (central Jordan), the king of the Moabites, Balak, summoned Balaam the prophet to curse the Israelites: "... *Look, a people has come from Egypt. See, they cover the face of the earth, and are settling next to me! Therefore please come at once, curse this people for me, for they are too mighty for me. Perhaps I shall be able to defeat them and drive them out of the land, for I know that he whom you bless is blessed, and he whom you curse is cursed"* (Num. 22:5–6).

God answered Balaam with these words: *"You shall not go with them; you shall not curse the people, for they are blessed"* (Num. 22:12).

Balaam, instead of cursing the Israelites, prophesied the coming Messiah: *"I see Him, but not now; I behold Him, but not near; a Star shall come out of Jacob [Israel]; a Scepter [Messiah] shall rise out of Israel, and batter the brow of Moab, and destroy all the sons of tumult [reference to the Arab people that came from Esau's marriages to Gentile idol-worshiping wives]"* (Num 24:17).

"And Edom [southern Jordan] shall be a possession; Seir also, his enemies, shall be a possession, while Israel does valiantly. Out of Jacob, One [Messiah] shall have dominion, and destroy the remains of the city" (Num. 24:18).

"Then he looked on Amalek, and he took up his oracle and said: 'Amalek was first among the nations, but shall be last until he perishes'" (Num. 24:20).

Balaam prophesied that Amalek would be called the first of the nations, for the Amalekites were the first foe to draw blood with the freed Israelites.

Then he prophesied that Amalek would be the last (antichrist), by reaffirming the words of Moses in Exodus 17:16: *"Because the LORD has sworn: the LORD will have war with Amalek from generation to generation."*

1,000 BC: Saul Is Appointed King

Samuel also said to Saul, "The Lord sent me to anoint you king over His people, over Israel. Now therefore, heed the voice of the words of the Lord. Thus says the Lord of hosts: 'I will punish Amalek for what he did to Israel, how he ambushed him on the way when he came up from Egypt. Now go and attack Amalek, and utterly destroy all that they have, and do not spare them. But kill both man and woman, infant and nursing child, ox and sheep, camel and donkey.'"

—1 Samuel 15:1–3

The Command to Kill the Amalekites

The command to kill an entire nation and their cattle was not new. God required the Israelites to do so for their protection when they encountered the Canaanite nations to ensure fulfillment of the coming Messiah. As the Israelites' second generation was entering the Promised Land and had established itself and won victory over its surrounding neighbors, they were reminded of their duty to their descendants to destroy the Amalekites.

"So Saul gathered the people together and numbered them in Telaim, two hundred thousand foot soldiers and ten thousand men of Judah. And Saul came to a city of Amalek, and lay in wait in the valley" (1 Sam. 15:4).

However, Saul had compassion on the Kenites who dwelled there and warned them of the coming onslaught. After the Kenites departed, *"Saul attacked the Amalekites, from Havilah all the way to Shur, which is east of Egypt. He also took Agag, king of the Amalekites, alive and utterly destroyed all the people with the edge of the sword. But Saul and the people spared Agag and the best of the sheep, the oxen, the fatlings, the lambs, and all that was good, and were unwilling to utterly destroy them. But everything despised and worthless, that they utterly destroyed"* (1 Sam. 15:7–9).

Saul Is Rejected as King

"Now the word of the Lord came to Samuel, saying, 'I greatly regret that I have set up Saul as king, for he has turned back from following Me, and has not performed My commandments.' And it grieved Samuel, and he cried out to the Lord all night" (1 Sam. 15:10–11).

"So Samuel said: 'Has the Lord as great delight in burnt offerings and sacrifices, as in obeying the voice of the Lord? Behold, to obey is better than sacrifice, and to heed than the fat of rams. For rebellion is as the sin of witchcraft, and stubbornness is as iniquity and idolatry. Because you have rejected the word of the Lord, He also has rejected you from being king' " (1 Sam. 15:22–23).

Agag Lives: The Bloodline Spreads

"The Amalekites had their origin within the Edomites, being descendants of Esau. They are often associated with Edom (Esau), living in the same area as Edom (Mt. Seir, southern Jordan). Their traditional territory was Transjordan between Babylon and the Gulf of Aqaba. The Edomites and Amalekites were enemies of Israel."[16]

Since both tribes were descendants of Esau, they were of great historical importance as descendants of both Isaac and Abraham. Despite their shared ancestry with the Israelites, the tribes lived in almost perpetual conflict and still do today. As far back as their journey through Sinai, Edom threatened the Israelites with "a mighty hand" and refused to allow them to pass through their territory en route to the Promised Land (Num. 20:20–21).

400 BC, Amalekites in Persia

Six hundred years after King Saul spared King Agag the Amalekite, his descendants had assimilated into Persia (Iran), and one who rose to prominence there was Haman, the Agagite, from the book of Esther. He was a noble and vizier to King Ahasuerus (Xerxes).

The evil bloodline that God had sworn to fight against in every generation (Ex. 17:16) was on the move. The same hatred that Amalek displayed, the same self-loathing of Jewish blood, and the same satanic effort to eliminate every Jew on earth were evident in Haman.

Nazi Amalekites

The Nazis and Adolf Hitler have frequently been referred to as Amalekites. A prominent nineteenth- and early-twentieth-century rabbi, Rabbi Yosef Chaim Sonnenfeld, claimed, upon Kaiser Wilhelm's visit to Palestine in 1898 three decades before Hitler's rise to power, that he had a tradition from his teachers that the Germans were descended from the ancient Amalekites. Rabbi Sonnenfeld searched out Amalek and recognized Esau's spirit in the Nazi regime. Likewise, Israeli president Itzhak Ben-Zvi, in 1962, when he responded to a request for clemency by Adolf Eichmann's wife, quoted Samuel's words to Agag, king of the

Amalekites: *"As your sword bereaved women, so will your mother be bereaved among women"* [1 Sam. 15:33].[17]

Palestinians as Amalekites

The similarities of the Palestinian people today in Judea and Samaria (West Bank) to their Edomite ancestors are remarkable. They are descendants of Abraham through the line of Esau and his Gentile (idol-worshiping) marriages. They display a fierce *self-loathing* of their partial Jewish heritage and an insatiable desire to wipe the Jews off the face of the earth.

Jimmy DeYoung, writing in 2006 on his website Prophecy Today, said:

> The prophet Malachi records that God says the borders of the people of Amalek, the Palestinians of today, would be the borders of wickedness; that's Malachi 1:4. Ezekiel says that the Amalekites will kill the Jews in the Last Days and try to take their land from them; that's Ezekiel 35. Jeremiah says that the Amalekites will be destroyed and be as if they had never been; Jeremiah 49:18. . . . Though the rabbi's call to annihilate Palestinian murderers is indeed shocking, the prophet Obadiah says that's exactly what will happen at the coming of the Messiah, Jesus Christ.[18]

Remember What the Amalekites did to you

Of the 613 mitzvot (commandments) followed by Orthodox Jews, three referred to the Amalekites: to remember what the Amalekites did to the Jews, to not forget what the Amalekites did to the Jews, and to destroy the Amalekites utterly.

The memory of Amalek has been a terrifying reminder to Jews over the millennia. In Jewish tradition, the Amalekites came to represent the archetypal enemy of the Jews.

Chapter 4

THE BABYLONIAN CAPTIVITY BEGINS

The Jews had been warned in 1400 BC by Moses who wrote in Leviticus 26:34–35: *"Then the land shall enjoy its Sabbaths as long as it lies desolate and you are in your enemies' land; then the land shall rest and enjoy its Sabbaths. As long as it lies desolate it shall rest—for the time it did not rest on your Sabbaths when you dwelt in it."*

Later Isaiah and Jeremiah had very specific warnings:

> " 'Behold, the days are coming when all that is in your house, and all that your fathers have laid up in store to this day shall be carried to Babylon, nothing shall be left,' says the Lord" (Isa. 39:6, 750 BC).

> "And the whole land shall be a desolation and a horror, and these nations shall serve the king of Babylon seventy years" (Jer. 25:11, 620 BC).

God's patience had run out on the disobedience of the Jews. He had instructed them to let the land rest every seventh year, even promising them a triple harvest in the sixth year. But for 490 years, or seventy sabbaticals, the land was not allowed the Sabbath rest. Because of this transgression, God permitted His children to be taken captive for seventy years to let the land rest. This was a dark day in Israel's history.

"In the third year of the reign of Jehoiakim king of Judah, Nebuchadnezzar king of Babylon came to Jerusalem and besieged it" (Dan. 1:1).

The Jews were taken out of Israel into captivity in three different waves. The first group, which was taken into captivity in 605 BC, caused a power vacuum in Jerusalem. The temple had been destroyed as well as the city walls, leaving Jerusalem open to entry by other tribes.

The second group was taken in 597 BC (sixth century). The third and final group, Judah, the southern kingdom, was taken in 586 BC, leaving the land almost devoid of people and cattle.

Obadiah's Warning

At the same time, the descendants of Esau were pushed out of their ancestral homeland in Mount Seir, southern Jordan, by a tribe known as the Nabateans. Unable to go due west to take on the more powerful Egyptians, the Edomites traveled northwest and settled in the lush pasturelands of Judea during the Babylonian captivity of the Jews. Due to the preponderance of Edomites, the Romans named the area to the south of Judea "Idumea."[19]

God's displeasure with these descendants of Esau was spoken through the prophet: *"On the day you [Esau's descendants] stood aloof while strangers carried off his wealth and foreigners entered his gates and cast lots for Jerusalem, you were like one of them. You should not gloat over your brother [Jacob's descendants] in the day of his misfortune, nor rejoice over the people of Judah in the day of their destruction, nor boast so much in the day of their trouble"* (Obad. 1:11–12).

The Babylonian Captivity Ends

The Jews returned to Israel in the same way they were taken captive: in three different groups. In 538 BC, the first group of Jews left Babylon under the leadership of Zerubbabel. There were 49,897 people in that group.[20]

By 516 BC, twenty-two years after their return, they had rebuilt the temple. However, the walls of the city still lay in rubble.

In 458 BC, Ezra led a group of 1,800 men (5,500 to 6,000 including women and children) back to Jerusalem.[21]

Twelve years after Ezra's return to the Holy Land, a third group returned from Persia with Nehemiah. He had received permission from King Artaxerxes in 445 BC (beginning the seventy weeks' prophecy of Daniel 9:24–27) to return to Jerusalem and rebuild the walls. There were 42,360 souls (or 125,000–130,000 total) in the city at that time, and they rebuilt the walls in fifty-two days (Neh. 7:66–73).

The Returning Jews Intermarry

In Deuteronomy 7:1-4 Moses warned the Jews when they came into the Promised Land to *"conquer and utterly destroy the Hittites and the Girgashites and the Amorites and the Canaanites and the Perizzites and the Hivites and the Jebusites. "You shall make no treaty with them, and show them no mercy. Do not intermarry with them. Do not give your daughters to their sons or take their daughters for your sons, for they will turn your children away from following me to serve other gods, and the LORD's anger will burn against you and will quickly destroy you."*

But that is not what happened. Ezra 9 records that the returning Jews indeed married the Canaanites, the same tribe that was recorded in Genesis 36:2 *"Esau took his wives from the women of Canaan."* And they married the Hittites, Perizzites, Jebusites, Ammonites, Moabites, Egyptians and Amorites.

Ezra, distraught for this violation of God's commands, prayed to the God of Israel and made a covenant to send the pagan wives and children away. However, the bloodline of Esau was already in the children of these unlawful marriages and spread throughout Judea.

God meant for the Jews to be a separate and holy people chosen from all the peoples on the face of the earth to be His people, His treasured possession.

Flavius Josephus Confirms Edomite Occupation in Southern Judea

"That country is also called Judea, and the people Jews; and this name is given also to as many as embrace their religion

[Judaism], though of other nations. But then upon what foundation so good a governor as Hyrcanus [grandson of Mattathias patriarch of the Maccabees, a family of Judahite patriots of 2nd and 1st centuries B.C.] took upon himself to compel these Idumeans [Edomites] either to become Jews or to leave their country, deserves great consideration. I suppose it was because they had been long ago driven out of the land of Edom, and had seized upon and possessed the tribe of Simeon [their land not the people], and all the southern part of the tribe of Judah which was the peculiar inheritance of the true God without idolatry."[22]

Idumea Also Called Bosra, or Bozrah

There were no natural boundaries between Idumea and Judea, so the borders were always in flux. Idumea was also referred to in Mark's gospel at the time of Jesus: *"And a great multitude from Galilee followed Him, and from Judea and Jerusalem and **Idumea** and beyond the Jordan; and those from Tyre and Sidon, a great multitude, when they heard how many things He was doing, came to Him"* (Mark 3:7–8, emphasis added).

The Ammonites had moved into Samaria (West Bank) from the northern part of Jordan, and the Edomites from the southern part. By the time of the birth of Jesus, many Jews had intermarried with both the Ammonites and Edomites, who were hostile toward the Jews from the northern kingdom.

At the trial of Jesus, two distinct groups of Jews can be seen. 1. The Pharisees, Sadducees, and scribes who were from Judea and part Edomite, stirred the people of Judea to call for the release of Barabbas and the death of Jesus at the hands of Pilate.

2. There were multitudes of Jews, mainly from the north in Galilee, who had followed Jesus throughout His ministry and called Him Messiah on Palm Sunday, saying, *"Blessed is He who comes in the name of the Lord"* (Matt. 21:9).

The Edomite Blood Moves North

The fifth century BC was known for the Greco-Persian wars that continued all the way to the rise of Alexander in 323 BC. These wars were a perfect fit for the mercenary Edomites, who were known as fierce sword-wielding warriors.

http://en.wikipedia.org/wiki/File:First_century_palestine.gif *Original uploader was Andrew c a\t en.wikipedia*

They were conscripted and recruited into these armies, spreading Esau's blood from Israel east to Persia (Iran) and north to Lebanon, Syria, Turkey (Chazars), and Russia/Ukraine (Scythians).

The Edomite soldiers then sailed, along with the Assyrians, to Greece and Rome. The ancient Jews called Rome "Bosra," a form of the word *Bozrah*, the first Edomite capital in Seir.

The nineteenth century theologian and Bible scholar Adam Clarke, in his commentary on Isaiah 34, quotes medieval rabbi David Kimchi, "Kimchi says, 'This chapter points out the future destruction of Rome, which is here called Bosra; for Bosra was a great city of the Edomites. Now the major part of the Romans are Edomites, who profess the law of Jesus. The Emperor Caesar . . . was an Edomite, and so were all the emperors after him.' "[23]

> For My sword shall be bathed in heaven; indeed it shall come down on **Edom**, and on the people of My curse, for judgment. The sword of the LORD is filled with blood; it is made overflowing with fatness, with the blood of lambs and goats, with the fat of the kidneys of rams. For the LORD has a sacrifice in Bozrah, and a great slaughter in the land of **Edom**. The wild oxen shall come down with them, and the young bulls with the mighty bulls; their land shall be soaked with blood, and their dust saturated with fatness, for it is the day of the LORD's vengeance, the year of recompense for the cause of Zion.
>
> —Isaiah 34:5–8, emphasis added

In Matthew Henry's commentary on the book of Isaiah, we find his thoughts regarding the above verses: "God's sword is bathed in heaven, in His counsel and decree, in His justice and power. . . . It will come down **upon Idumea, the people of God's curse,** *the people that lie under His curse and are by it doomed to destruction*" (emphasis added).[24]

Jack Kinsella, in the Omega Letter, November 2006, wrote:

> "That Obadiah's prophecies extend into the present day is evidenced by his references in verse 15-17 to the

61

Day of the Lord, the recovery of the Temple Mount and references to land not yet recovered by Israel. Obadiah's prophecy begins with the ancient Edomites and tracks their physical and spiritual descendants to the last days.

["For the day of the Lord upon all the nations *is* near; As you have done, it shall be done to you; Your reprisal shall return upon your own head. For as you drank on My holy mountain, *So* shall all the nations drink continually; Yes, they shall drink, and swallow, And they shall be as though they had never been.

"But on Mount Zion there shall be deliverance, And there shall be holiness; The house of Jacob shall possess their possessions.

The house of Jacob shall be a fire, And the house of Joseph a flame; But the house of Esau *shall be* stubble; They shall kindle them and devour them And no survivor shall *remain* of the house of Esau," For the Lord has spoken."]

… The most compelling Scriptural evidence to identify the Edomites is found in Ezekiel 36:5. [… 'Surely I have spoken in My burning jealousy against the rest of the nations and against all Edom, who gave My land to themselves as a possession, with wholehearted joy and spiteful minds, in order to plunder its open country."][25]

Parallel Prophecies: Obadiah and Jeremiah Confirm
Judgment on Esau

Jeremiah and Obadiah confirm that Esau would be deceptive and must be searched out:

> But I will strip Esau bare; I will uncover his hiding places, so that he cannot conceal himself.

—Jeremiah: 49:10

> Oh, how Esau shall be searched out! How his hidden treasures shall be sought after!

—Obadiah 1:6

No other person in the Bible is judged as harshly as Esau:

> Edom also shall be astonishment; everyone who goes by it will be astonished and will hiss at all its plagues.

—Jeremiah 49:17

> And no survivor shall remain of the house of Esau.

—Obadiah 1:18

Edom the Final Enemy

Isaiah, writing 750 years before the birth of Jesus Christ, gave us the answer as to why Jesus' robe will be bloodied when He appears in His second coming:

Who is this coming from **Edom**, from Bozrah, with his garments stained crimson? Who is this, robed in splendor, striding forward in the greatness of his strength?

"It is I, proclaiming victory, mighty to save."

Why are your garments red, like those of one treading the winepress?

"I have trodden the winepress alone; from the nations no one was with me. I trampled them in my anger and trod them down in my wrath; their blood spattered my garments, and I stained all my clothing."

—Isaiah 63:1–3, emphasis added

On His way to save Israel, the Lord will take vengeance on Edom, putting an end to the hatred between Jacob (Jew) and Esau (Arab). The apostle John, reaffirming Isaiah on the glorious return of the Lord Jesus Christ, gives a stunning answer to Isaiah's questions, *Who is this?* and *Why are Your garments red?*

He is dressed in a robe dipped in blood, and his name is the Word of God. The armies of heaven were following him, riding on white horses and dressed in fine linen, white and clean. Coming out of his mouth is a sharp sword with which to strike down the nations. He will rule them with an iron scepter. He treads the winepress of the fury of the wrath of God Almighty. On his robe and on his thigh he has this name written: King of Kings and Lord of Lords.

—Revelation 19:13–16 NIV

Note that the armies of saints have no blood on their fine linen robes. Jesus went to Bozrah alone. The Bridegroom would never take His bride (church) into battle. Then, in Revelation 19:20, the final Amalek is thrown into the bottomless pit.

The Betrayal of Jesus

During the ministry of Christ, only one of His disciples, the one who betrayed Him, was from Judea, Judas Iscariot. The other eleven disciples were Galileans from the north.

Judas is said to be from Kerioth (John 6:71), a town close to Hebron in the south of Judea, hence, his name, Iscariot. He is the only apostle whose place of birth is always associated with his name. In the listings of the twelve apostles in the New Testament, Judas's name is always last.

Judas was an Edomite (part-Jewish, part-Gentile blood), as were the scribes, Pharisees, and Sadducees, which explains the harsh treatment given them by Jesus. In Matthew's gospel, on more than one occasion, Jesus referred to these lawyers and teachers of the law as evil, hypocrites, and a brood of vipers: *"O generation of **vipers**, how can you, being evil, speak good things? For out of the abundance of the heart the mouth speaks"* (Matt. 12:34, emphasis added).

It's interesting to remember here that Esau, according to the Talmud, was born with the mark of the figure of the **serpent**.[26]

The Search for Antichrist

We learned from Obadiah that Esau will be searched out. We learned from Moses that God has sworn to have war with Amalek through each generation. These verses have been leading our search for the final antichrist through nine predecessors. Each of these had partial Jewish blood.

In Amalek we found the same indwelling evil spirit of Esau, which will prevail in the final Man of Sin. It was Amalek who drew the first blood. It was Amalek's self-loathing of his Jewish blood that the LORD has sworn to avenge.

Knowing that *salvation is from the Jews* (John 4:22), Satan tried to prevent the Messiah's birth by attempting to eradicate every Jew.

It will be a future Amalek indwelt by Satan who will confirm a *seven-year peace treaty with Israel* and who, after a brief peace, will unleash such evil that has never been seen before. The chapters to follow will show that Amalek's hatred of God's children was manifested in men who had an insatiable desire to wipe out an entire race of people.

"That the name of Israel may be remembered no more" (Ps. 83:4).

CHAPTER 5

HAMAN THE AGAGITE: ANTICHRIST #3

Haman was an Agagite, a descendant of Agag, king of Amalek. An Agagite is an Amalekite, and Amalek was a descendant of Esau.

Haman's lineage is given in the Targum Sheni as follows: "Haman the son of Hammedatha the Agagite, son of Srach, son of Buza, son of Iphlotas, son of Dyosef, son of Dyosim, son of Prome, son of Ma'dei, son of Bla'akan, son of Intimrom, son of Harirom, son of Sh'gar, son of Nigar, son of Farmashta, son of Vayezatha, son of Agag, son of Sumki, son of Amalek, *son of the concubine of Eliphaz, firstborn son of Esau.*"[27] Emphasis added

Haman was a fifth-century-BC noble and vizier (high official) of the Persian Empire under King Ahasuerus, traditionally identified as Xerxes. Haman, also known as "Haman the Evil," desired to wipe out all the Jews of Israel, having inherited the same long-standing tradition of Amalek and Esau. He was the main antagonist in the book of Esther.

The biblical book of Esther is set in the third year of Ahasuerus, king of Persia.

King Ahasuerus (Xerxes) had banished Queen Vashti for not complying with his demand that she show herself before a drunken orgy of the king's guests. The king grew lonely, and a beauty pageant was held to find the king a new queen. At the coaxing of her cousin Mordecai, who was the leader of the Jews at that time, Esther reluctantly entered the competition, hiding her Jewish ancestry. To Esther's surprise, she was selected queen of Persia.

We pick up the story of Esther in the fifth century (485 BC) near the end of the Babylonian captivity. The holy temple that had stood in Jerusalem was destroyed in 586 BC, and the Jews were subjects of the mighty Persian Empire, which extended over 127 lands.

"After these things King Ahasuerus promoted Haman, the son of Hammedatha the Agagite, and advanced him and set his seat above all the princes who were with him" (Est. 3:1).

Haman was a high official; in effect, the prime minister. After Esther became queen of Persia, her cousin Mordecai would not bow down to Haman, who was known to have an idol hanging from a chain around his neck. Mordecai was, in fact, very loyal to the king and sat in the king's gate, or council, but he would not submit to honor Haman.

Mordecai's refusal to bow to Haman, an Amalekite, was not due to a stubborn or proud spirit in Mordecai. It was due to his faithfulness to God's attitude toward Amalekites.

Because of his faith in God, Mordecai might have feared God's wrath upon him if he had bowed to Haman. It was Mordecai's great faith in God's words that he would risk his life by refusing to bow before an Amalekite, even if the Amalekite had become a man of great political power. Mordecai trusted the power of God's curse to be greater than Haman's ranking given him by the Persian king.

"And when Haman saw that Mordecai did not bow down or do obeisance to him, Haman was filled with fury. But he disdained to lay hands on Mordecai alone. So, as they had made known to him the people of Mordecai, Haman sought to destroy all the Jews, the people of Mordecai, throughout the whole kingdom of Ahasuerus" (Est. 3:5–6).

> Then Haman said to King Ahasuerus, "There is a certain people scattered and dispersed among the people in all the provinces of your kingdom; their laws are different from all other people's, and they do not keep the king's laws. Therefore it is not fitting for the king to let them remain. If it pleases the king, let a decree be written that they be destroyed, and I will pay ten thousand talents of silver into the hands of those who do the work, to bring it into the king's treasuries."

> So the king took his signet ring from his hand and gave it to Haman, the son of Hammedatha the Agagite, the enemy of the Jews. And the king said to Haman, "The

money and the people are given to you, to do with them as seems good to you."

—Esther 3:8–11

For Such a Time as This

Now Esther, who was Jewish, had withheld her heritage from the king. And Mordecai sent a message to Esther: "Do not think in your heart that you will escape in the king's palace any more than all the other Jews. For if you remain completely silent at this time, relief and deliverance will arise for the Jews from another place, but you and your father's house will perish. Yet who knows whether you have come to the kingdom for such a time as this?"

Then Esther told them to reply to Mordecai: "Go, gather all the Jews who are present in Shushan, and fast for me; neither eat nor drink for three days, night or day. My maids and I will fast likewise. And so I will go to the king, which is against the law; and if I perish, I perish!"

So Mordecai went his way and did according to all that Esther commanded him.

—Esther 4:13–17

Esther's Request to the King

After three days of fasting, Esther, dressed in the queen's garb, entered Ahasuerus's chambers. Immediately the king extended his scepter. "What is it?" Ahasuerus asked. "What is your request?"

Esther asked that the king and Haman come attend a feast that she had prepared for the king that day. The king and Haman quickly went to the feast. After they finished eating, the king asked Esther what her desire was. She replied that she wished Haman and the king would attend another feast the next day—then she would reveal her request. Haman left the party quite proud of himself. On his way home, he passed Mordecai at the gate, who still refused to bow.

Upon arriving home, Haman boasted to his wife, Zeresh, about his second invitation from the queen, but how Mordecai still refused to bow to him.

"Then his wife Zeresh and all his friends said to him, 'Let a gallows be made, fifty cubits high, and in the morning suggest to the king that Mordecai be hanged on it; then go merrily with the king to the banquet.' And the thing pleased Haman; so he had the gallows made" (Est. 5:14).

The King Learns of Mordecai's Loyalty

That night the king could not sleep. So one was commanded to bring the book of the records of the chronicles; and they were read before the king. And it was found written that Mordecai had told of Bigthana and

Teresh, two of the king's eunuchs who had guarded the doorway, had conspired to assassinate King Xerxes.

"What honor or dignity has been bestowed on Mordecai for this?" And the king's servants who attended him said, "Nothing has been done for him." That very moment Haman entered the king's court, intending to ask the king's permission to hang Mordecai. Before Haman could say a word, Ahasuerus addressed him: "What should be done for the man the king delights to honor?"

Haman, who was certain that the king wished to honor him, responded: "Bring royal garments and a royal horse. And let one of the king's nobles dress the man and lead him on the horse through the city streets, proclaiming before him, 'So is done for the man whom the king wishes to honor!' "

Ahasuerus responded, "Now go get the garments and the horse and do so for Mordecai the Jew!"

—Esther 6:1–10

So Haman took the robe and the horse, arrayed Mordecai and led him on horseback through the city square, and proclaimed before him, "Thus shall it be done to the man whom the king delights to honor!"

Afterward Mordecai went back to the king's gate. But Haman hurried to his house, mourning and with his head covered. When Haman told his wife Zeresh and all his friends everything that had happened to him, his wise men and his wife Zeresh said to him, "If Mordecai, before whom you have begun to fall, is of Jewish descent, you will not prevail against him but will surely fall before him."

While they were still talking with him, the king's eunuchs came, and hastened to bring Haman to the banquet which Esther had prepared.

—Esther 6:11–14

Esther Intervenes

So the king and Haman went to dine with Queen Esther. And on the second day, at the banquet of wine, the king again said to Esther, "What is your petition, Queen Esther? It shall be granted you. And what is your request, up to half the kingdom? It shall be done!"

Then Queen Esther answered and said, "If I have found favor in your sight, O king, and if it pleases the king, let my life be given me at my petition, and my people at my request. For we have been sold, my people and I, to be destroyed, to be killed, and to be annihilated.

Had we been sold as male and female slaves, I would have held my tongue, although the enemy could never compensate for the king's loss."

So King Ahasuerus answered and said to Queen Esther, "Who is he, and where is he, who would dare presume in his heart to do such a thing?"

And Esther said, "The adversary and enemy is Haman."

So Haman was terrified before the king and queen.

—Esther 7:1–6

Haman Is Hanged

Now Harbonah, one of the eunuchs, said to the king, "Look! The gallows, fifty cubits high, which Haman made for Mordecai, who spoke good on the king's behalf, is standing at the house of Haman."

Then the king said, "Hang him on it!"

So they hanged Haman on the gallows that he had prepared for Mordecai.

—Esther 7:9–10

On that day, Haman's estate was given to Esther, and Mordecai was appointed prime minister in place of Haman. Yet Esther was not satisfied. Haman was dead, but his evil decree was still in effect. According to Persian law, once a king issued a decree, it could not be rescinded.

Haman's Sons Are Hanged

The king gave Mordecai and Esther permission to write a decree that countermanded Haman's edict. The new decree granted the Jews permission to defend themselves against their enemies. On the thirteenth of Adar that year, the Jews throughout the Persian Empire mobilized and killed the enemies who had wanted to kill them. In Shushan, among the dead were Haman's ten sons.

Esther asked the king's permission for the Jews to have one more day to destroy their enemy, and the king granted her wish. On the fourteenth of Adar, the Jews of Shushan killed more of their enemies and also hung Haman's sons even though they were already dead. They also rested and made it a day of feasting and gladness (Est. 9:11-17). This holiday, called "Purim", is the most joyous holiday on the Jewish calendar.

The Rest of the Story

The similarities and parallels of Purim to the Nuremberg trials of 1946 and the Six-Day War of 1967 are remarkable:

1. Throughout history, God always raises up someone to save the Jewish people from total annihilation. Even though the Edomites, Amalekites, Moabites, and Hittites as a people group have disappeared from the pages of history, their

bloodlines through their descendants are still here today. But, God has preserved the Israelites as His (chosen) people group, and will continue to do so to the Millennial reign of Christ.

2. The Jewish army, 2,500 years ago, preempted the attack of the Persian army against overwhelming odds and defeated them. The Israeli army in 1967 preempted the war with Egypt, Jordan, and Syria; Israel captured the West Bank, East Jerusalem, the Gaza Strip, the Golan Heights, and the Sinai Peninsula in an incredible victory that stunned the world.

3. In approximately 520 BC, after the Jewish people defeated the Persians, Queen Esther asked for Haman's ten sons to be hanged. In 1946, the Nuremberg trials pronounced twelve of Hitler's generals guilty and sentenced them to hang. Martin Bormann was killed prior to the trials, and Herman Goering committed suicide hours before the hangings. That left ten generals. (In 1945, the method of military execution was firing squad. There was no explanation for the change of venue).

On October 16, 1946, Hitler's ten generals were executed in the same manner as Haman's ten sons. That day fell on the seventh day of Sukkot, the Feast of Tabernacles, and is called Hoshana Rabbah.

Sukkot is the Feast of Booths, when God will gather with His people to "tabernacle" with Him. Christians believe that this feast will one day be the fulfillment of the Davidic covenant when Jesus Christ returns to set up His thousand-year reign on earth.

Yom Kippur is the day that God's judgments are determined, and Hoshana Rabbah is the day that judgments are delivered. It was on Hoshana Rabbah that Hitler's generals were hung.

And now, for the rest of the story . . . One of Hitler's generals, Julius Streicher, who had to be dragged to the gallows, screamed to the witnesses, "Purim Fest 1946!"[28]

Chapter 6

ANTIOCHUS EPIPHANES: ANTICHRIST #4

When you see standing in the holy place "the abomination that causes desolation," spoken of through the prophet Daniel—let the reader understand—then let those who are in Judea flee to the mountains.

—Matthew 24:15–16 NIV

323 BC: Alexander's Empire Collapses

"Then a mighty king shall arise, who shall rule with great dominion, and do according to his [own] will" (Dan. 11:3).

Daniel wrote these words around 550 BC, over two hundred years before the birth of the mighty king mentioned above. That king would be Alexander the Great, unquestionably one of the most brilliant generals in history.

Alexander extended the Greek Empire until there were no other kingdoms left to conquer. In a dual prophecy, Daniel 7:8 said that there would be another king, who would do according to his own will. He would speak *pompous words* against the Most High. His name is Antichrist.

"And when he has arisen, his kingdom shall be broken up and divided toward the four winds of heaven, but not among his posterity nor according to his dominion with which he ruled; for his kingdom shall be uprooted, even for others besides these" (Dan. 11:4).

After his death at age thirty-three from alcoholism and depression, Alexander's kingdom was divided among his four generals, fulfilling Daniel's prophecy. Neither Alexander's brother Philip, nor an illegitimate son named Hercules, nor a yet-to-be born son, would inherit his empire since all three were killed.

The four divisions were as follows:

Cassander: Macedonia, Greece, and Asia Minor

Lysimachus: Southeast Europe, Bulgaria

Ptolemy: Egypt, king of the south, Daniel 11:5

Seleucus: Syria, king of the north, Daniel 11:6

Following the death of Alexander, who overthrew the Medo-Persian Empire in 331 BC, the south fell to the new Ptolemaic rulers of Egypt, while Syria was incorporated into the Seleucid Empire of the north. During the first century BC, all four kingdoms were eventually incorporated into the Roman Republic.

The Edomites and Greeks

The Babylonian captivity that began in 586 BC (sixth century) created a power vacuum in Judea. The Edomites who dwelled in the Greek-inspired city of Petra (southern Jordan) were forced out by the Nabateans and moved into southern Israel's (Judah) lush grazing lands.

The fifth century BC was known for the Persian-Greek wars that continued all the way to the rise of Alexander in 336 BC. These wars were a perfect fit for the mercenary Edomites, known as fierce sword-wielding warriors, who made excellent recruits for the Greek armies.

By the fourth and third centuries BC, the Edomites had inter-married with the returning Israelites, spreading the Esau bloodline through Judah. The Edomites moved from Israel north to Syria, Turkey, and sailed along with the Assyrians to Greece and Rome.

Antiochus Epiphanes Becomes King of Syria

http://commons.wikimedia.org/wiki/File:Seleucid-Empire_200bc-smaller.jpg by Thomas Lessman

"He will be succeeded by a contemptible person who has not been given the honor of royalty. He will invade the kingdom when its people feel secure, and he will seize it through intrigue" (Dan. 11:21 NIV).

The great prophet Daniel, writing over three hundred years before the birth of Antiochus, gave us the details about the rise of the evil king and, in a dual prophecy, a look at how the final antichrist will rise to power—by first coming in peace. Antiochus used his manipulative skills, treachery, and deceit (an Edomite trait) to acquire the crown over his nephew Demetrius, the rightful heir, whose father was mysteriously poisoned.

In a foreshadowing, the apostle John wrote in Revelation 6:2, *"And I looked, and behold, a white horse. He who sat on it had a bow; and a crown was given to him, and he went out conquering and to conquer."* The bow with no arrows is a symbol of antichrist coming in the name of (short-lived) peace.

By 188 BC, Syria had already been incorporated into the Seleucid Empire. Antiochus, son of the Persian-born Antiochus the Great, ruled from 175 BC to 164 BC.

A Shadow of the Final Antichrist

Antiochus Epiphanes is widely recognized by prophecy scholars as a precursor to the final antichrist, or the little horn of Daniel 8:9: *"And out of one of them [one of four generals, Seleucus] came a little horn [an antichrist figure] which grew exceedingly great toward the south, toward the east, and toward the Glorious Land [Israel]."*

Antiochus regarded himself as Zeus, the Greek god; hence, his self-given title *Epiphanes*, meaning "manifestation of God" or "illustrious one." His diabolical plan was to Hellenize Israel and thereby eradicate Judaism. He established numerous Greek cities throughout his empire.

From the apocryphal book of 1 Maccabees 1:11–12: "And there came out of them *a wicked root*, Antiochus the Epiphanes who had been hostage in Rome. In those days went there out of Israel wicked men [Edomites who had intermarried with Judahites], who persuaded many, saying, Let us go and make a covenant with the heathen that are round about us: for since we departed from them we have had much sorrow" (emphasis added).

"Then certain of the people were so forward herein, that they went to the king, who gave them licence to do after the ordinances of the heathen: Whereupon they built a place of exercise [gymnasium, center of athletic and intellectual life] at Jerusalem according to the customs of the heathen: And made themselves uncircumcised [made prepuces, folds of skin to cover their circumcision], *and forsook the holy covenant* [Abrahamic covenant sign of circumcision], and joined themselves to the heathen, and were sold to do mischief [evil]" (1 Macc. 1:14–16 KJV, emphasis added).

Note: Esau, as we have already seen, was the first of Abraham's household to abandon the covenant by refusing cir-cumcision, thereby making himself an enemy of God.

The First Abomination of Desolation

In 168 BC, Antiochus stepped up his campaign to crush Judaism so that all subjects in his vast empire, which included the land of Israel, would share the same culture and worship the same (Greek) gods. Times of terror and persecution befell the Jewish people. He quickly earned the nickname *Epimanes*, or "madman," a play on the word *Epiphanes*. Decreeing that studying Torah, observing the Sabbath, and circumcising Jewish boys were punishable by death, he sent Syrian overseers and soldiers to villages throughout Judea to enforce the edicts and force Jews to engage in idol worship. Many fled to the wilderness, but thousands died at the hands of the madman.

First-century historian Josephus: "Now Antiochus was not satisfied either with his unexpected taking the city [Jerusalem] or with its pillage, or with the great slaughter he had made there; but being overcome with his violent passions, and remembering what he had suffered during the siege, he compelled the Jews to dissolve the laws of their country, and to keep their infants uncircumcised, and to sacrifice swine's flesh upon the altar; against which they all opposed themselves, and the most approved among them were put to death."[29]

He marched into Jerusalem, and in a foreshadowing of the final abomination of desolation that will be carried out by the antichrist, he turned his attention to the Temple Mount (Dan. 11:31–32). Syrian soldiers hacked and smashed the porches and gates and stripped the temple of its golden vessels and treasures. On December 15, 158 BC, Antiochus erected an idol of Zeus on the holy altar. Ten days later on Zeus's birthday, December 25, he slaughtered a pig on the holy altar, desecrating its holiness with the blood of swine.

And he proudly entered into the sanctuary [Holy of Holies], and took away the golden altar, and the candlestick of light, and all the vessels thereof, and the table of proposition, and the pouring vessels, and the vials, and the little mortars of gold, and the veil, and the crowns, and the golden ornament that was before the temple: and he broke them all in pieces.

And he took the silver and gold, and the precious vessels: and he took the hidden treasures which he found: and when he had taken all away he departed into his own country.

And he made a great slaughter of men, and spoke very proudly. And there was great mourning in Israel, and in every place where they were.

And the princes and the ancients mourned, and the virgins and the young men were made feeble, and the beauty of the women was changed.

—1 Maccabees 1:18–28

Antiochus Establishes a Decree

Antiochus's decree included the following: he forbade sacrifices and atonements to be made in the temple of God; he prohibited the Sabbath and the festival days (Levitical feasts); the holy places and the holy people of Israel were to be profaned.

From 1 Maccabees 1:43–45: "And King Antiochus wrote to all his kingdom, that all the people should be one: and everyone should leave his own law. And all nations consented according to the word of King Antiochus. And many of Israel consented to his service, and they sacrificed to idols, and profaned the Sabbath."

Here is a most distinct sign of the evil spirit of Esau and the brutality of Amalek manifested in the Jews of southern Israel: "And they commanded the cities of Judah to sacrifice: Then *many of the people were gathered to them* that had forsaken the law of the Lord: and *they committed evils in the land*" (1 Macc. 1:55–56, emphasis added).

Antiochus's obsession against circumcision is reminiscent of Esau's refusal to be circumcised at age thirteen. This was clear rebellion against God's sign of covenant in Genesis 17:14: *"Any uncircumcised male, who has not been circumcised in the flesh, will be cut off from his people; he has broken My covenant."*

The Maccabean Revolt

On the fifteenth day of the month Casleu [December], in the hundred and forty-fifth year [167 BC], King Antiochus set up the abominable idol of desolation [statue of Zeus] upon the altar of God, and they built altars throughout all the cities of Judah round about.

And they burnt incense, and sacrificed at the doors of the houses, and in the streets.

And they cut in pieces, and burnt with fire the books of the law of God:

And every one with whom the books of the testament of the Lord were found, and whosoever observed the law of the Lord, they put to death, according to the edict of the king.

Thus by their power did they deal with the people of Israel, that were found in the cities month after month.

And on the five and twentieth day of the month [December 25] they sacrificed upon the altar of the idol that was over against the altar of God.

Now the women that circumcised their children were slain according to the commandment of King Antiochus.

And they hanged the children about their necks in all their houses: and those that had circumcised them, they put to death.

And many of the people of Israel determined with themselves, that they would not eat unclean things: and they chose rather to die than to be defiled with unclean meats.

And they would not break the holy law of God, and they were put to death:

And there was very great wrath upon the people.

—1 Maccabees 1:57–67

From verse 57 above, one of the many altars built to honor Zeus was in the town of Modin (seventeen miles northwest of Jerusalem). It was there that the soldiers ordered an aged priest, Mattathias, to offer a pig on the altar. After he refused, an apostate Jewish priest asked permission to offer the pig. In defiance, Mattathias ran a sword through the priest and a soldier, and together with his five sons, the revolt of the Maccabees began.

The Cleansing of the Temple

For three years, the siege of the Maccabees raged, until the Jews scored stunning victories at Beth-heron and Emmaus, opening the road to Jerusalem. They rebuilt the holy altar and rededicated it to the Lord exactly three years from the day it was defiled.

According to the Talmud, the Maccabees found one small case of unpolluted oil that still bore the unbroken seal of the high priest.[30] It was only one day's supply of oil for the golden lamp stand. Miraculously, the oil burned for eight days. The tradition of the eight days of Hanukkah began, a time of celebration and gifts. The story of Hanukkah is preserved in the books of 1 and 2 Maccabees.

Dual Prophecy: The Second Abomination of Desolation

In Daniel 9:27 NIV, the prophet tells us that in the last days before the return of Christ, there will be a second (dual prophecy) abomination of desolation performed by the final antichrist: *"He will confirm a covenant with many for one 'seven' [seven years]. In the middle of the 'seven' [forty-two months, or 3.5 years] he will put an end to [animal] sacrifice and offering. And at the [third] temple he will set up an abomination that causes desolation [declare himself God], until the end that is decreed is poured out on him."*

"And forces [satanic] shall be mustered by him, and they shall defile the sanctuary fortress; then they shall take away the daily sacrifices, and place there the abomination of desolation" (Dan. 11:31).

Antiochus committed the first abomination of desolation when in 168 BC he defied God and stood in the Holy of Holies in the Jewish temple and slaughtered an unclean animal. God turned this first abomination to good, as it led to the cleansing of the temple and the Jewish feast of Hanukkah.

The End of the Reign

The latter part of Antiochus's reign saw the further disintegration of the empire. The eastern areas remained nearly uncontrollable, as Parthians began to take over the Persian lands.

The Maccabean revolt in 167 BC led to an independent Jewish state. Efforts to deal with both the Parthians and the Jews proved fruitless, and Antiochus himself died during an expedition against the Parthians in 164 BC.

Conclusion

In Matthew 24:15, Jesus drew a parallel between the abomination of the second temple and the desecration of a future holy temple. End-time believers will know the final Amalek by the second abomination.

"Therefore when you see the 'abomination of desolation,' spoken of by Daniel the prophet, standing in the holy place (whoever reads, let him understand)."

CHAPTER 7

HEROD THE GREAT: ANTICHRIST #5

Herod was an Edomite, enmity to Israel was bred in the bone with him.

—Matthew Henry

Herod was half-Jewish and was descended from Abraham through Isaac and Esau rather than through Isaac and Jacob. Herod and family were considered to be Idumeans; this was a term employed by the Greeks and Romans for the country of Edom, or southern Israel south of Judea. Ancient Edom was located in the area of southern Jordan or Mount Seir (modern-day Petra). It is specifically noted as the place where Esau had made his home (Gen. 36:8; Josh. 24:4).

Migration into Idumea

Nomadic Nabateans migrated out of Arabia into Edom and drove the Edomites westward. Directly west of Edom were established routes of passage. Land there was historically more prosperous and resourceful than the land of Edom, which consisted of infertile deserts and jagged mountains.

Furthermore, the land bore a family association, after all, Esau was Jacob's brother. Hebron, 19 miles south of Jerusalem and 3400 ft. above sea level, became their new capital. It had been established 1500 years earlier and, unlike Jerusalem, was left intact as prime real estate after the Babylonian deportation under Nebuchadnezzar.

"When Nebuchadnezzar took Jerusalem, the Edomites sided with the Babylonians (Lam 4 21; Ezk 35:3-15; Ob vs 10-16), and during the absence of the Jews they advanced north and occupied all the Negeb and Southern Judaea as far as Hebron. Here they annoyed the Jews in Maccabean times until Judas expelled them from Southern Judaea (164 BC) and John Hyrcanus conquered their country and compelled them to become Jews (109 BC)."[31]

In the days the Babylonians carried away the Jews into captivity, the Edomites encouraged them, *"...Tear it down," they cried, "tear it down to its foundations!"* Psalm 137:7 NIV.

The book of Obadiah, written at the time of the Babylonian captivity, warned judgment against the Edomites for standing by while Jacob (Israel) was being taken captive by Babylon:

For violence against your brother Jacob, shame shall cover you, and you shall be cut off forever. In the day that you stood on the other side—in the day that strangers carried captive his forces, when foreigners entered his gates and cast lots for Jerusalem—even you were as one of them. But you should not have gazed on the day of your brother in the day of his captivity; nor should you have rejoiced over the children of Judah in the day of their destruction; nor should you have spoken proudly in the day of distress. You should not have entered the gate of My people in the day of their calamity. Indeed, you should not have gazed on their affliction in the day of their calamity, nor laid hands on their substance in the day of their calamity. You should not have stood at the crossroads to cut off those among them who escaped; nor should you have delivered up those among them who remained in the day of distress.

—Obadiah 1:10–14

Then God pronounced a future judgment: *"For the day of the Lord upon all the nations is near; as you have done* [to Israel]*, it shall be done to you; your reprisal shall return upon your own head"* (Obad. 1:15).

The prophet Ezekiel wrote of the inhabitants of Mount Seir:

"Behold, O Mount Seir, I am against you; I will stretch out My hand against you, and make you most desolate; I shall lay your cities waste, and you shall be desolate. Then you shall know that I am the Lord:

"Because you have had an ancient hatred, and have shed the blood of the children of Israel by the power of the sword at the time of their calamity, when their iniquity came to an end, therefore, as I live," says the Lord God, "I will prepare you for blood, and blood shall pursue you; since you have not hated blood, therefore blood shall pursue you.

"Thus I will make Mount Seir most desolate, and cut off from it the one who leaves and the one who returns. And I will fill its mountains with the slain; on your hills and in your valleys and in all your ravines those who are slain by the sword shall fall. I will make you perpetually desolate, and your cities shall be uninhabited; then you shall know that I am the Lord."

—Ezekiel 35:2–9

The fierceness of the descendants of Esau made excellent recruits for the conquering Greeks and Romans. Herod's father was an Idumean, and his mother was an Arab.

Herod was a political opportunist much like all of Rome's leaders, but he was also treacherous, evil, cruel, paranoid, and a perfect fit to come from the bloodline of Esau.

In 50 BC, the attitude in Rome was one of tolerance toward the Jews. The state religion was emperor worship, and their emperors were deified posthumously.

Flavius Josephus Confirms Herod's Bloodline

The Jewish historian Josephus (approximately AD 30–100) records that Esau's descendants inhabited the region of Idumea (Edom) at least two times in his writings:

> And these were the sons of Esau. Aliphaz had five legitimate sons: Theman, Omer, Saphus, Gotham, and Kanaz; for Amalek was not legitimate, but by a concubine, whose name was Thamna. These dwelt in that part of Idumea.[32]

> So he fell upon the Idumeans, the posterity of Esau, at Acrabattene, and slew a great many of them, and took their spoils.[33]

> Thus the Idumeans were considered to be the descendants of Esau.

In Book 14, Chapter 15, Par. 2, Josephus tells us that King Herod was an Idumean, confirming Herod the Great as a descendant of Esau: "But Antigonus, by way of reply to what Herod had caused to be proclaimed, and this before the Romans, and before Silo also, said that they would not do justly, if they gave the kingdom to Herod, who was no more than a private man, and an Idumean, i.e. a half Jew."[34]

Herod's Early Career

Herod's father, Antipater, appointed him the governor of Galilee, and his rise to power took place during the Roman civil war that would transform Rome from a republic into an empire ruled by the caesars, or emperors. In 44 BC, Julius Caesar was murdered by Brutus and Cassius, who were in turn defeated by Antony and Octavian in 42 BC.

The Battle of Actium in 31 BC was the final showdown between Octavian and Antony. Octavian emerged as the unrivaled victor, changing his name to Augustus and becoming the first Roman emperor.

Herod had originally sided with Antony but switched allegiance at the last minute and backed Octavian. His last-minute support for Octavian earned Herod confirmation as king of Israel.

With Herod's rise to power, the second wave of Edomites, under the protection of Rome, flooded into Judea in 37 BC.

Rome at this time was exploding in growth, and Herod became obsessed with massive construction projects. His building projects were in Palestine and included whole cities like Caesarea Maritima and Masada, as well as the rebuilding of Jericho. Most importantly, he rebuilt and expanded the temple of Solomon in Jerusalem, which is the reason it was called "Herod's temple."

In addition to receiving huge profits from agriculture, Herod imposed crushing taxes on the Jews in order to fund his grandiose buildings, including the temple.

Josephus Describes the Temple

"... Before these doors there was a veil of equal largeness with the doors. It was a Babylonian curtain, embroidered with blue, and fine linen, and scarlet, and purple, and of a contexture that was truly wonderful.

But the inmost part of the temple of all was of twenty cubits. This was also separated from the outer part by a veil. In this there was nothing at all. It was inaccessible and inviolable, and not to be seen by any; and was called the Holy of Holies.

Now the outward face of the temple in its front wanted nothing that was likely to surprise either men's minds or their eyes; for it was covered all over with plates of gold of great weight, and, at the first rising of the sun, reflected back a very fiery splendor, and made those who forced themselves to look upon it to turn their eyes away, just as they would have done at the sun's own rays. But this temple appeared to strangers, when they were coming to it at a distance, like a mountain covered with snow; for as to those parts of it that were not gilt, they were exceeding white."[35]

Herod saw fit, however, to place at the main entrance a huge Roman eagle, which the pious Jews saw as a sacrilege. A group of Torah students promptly smashed this emblem of idolatry and oppression, but Herod had them hunted down and in the last act of his life dragged the Jews in chains to his residence in Jericho, where they were burned alive.[36]

Herod and the Birth of Jesus

Now after Jesus was born in Bethlehem of Judea in the days of Herod the king, behold, wise men from the East came to Jerusalem, saying, "Where is He who has been born King of the Jews? For we have seen His star in the East and have come to worship Him."

When Herod the king heard this, he was troubled, and all Jerusalem with him. And when he had gathered all the chief priests and scribes of the people together, he inquired of them where the Christ was to be born.

So they said to him, "In Bethlehem of Judea, for thus it is written by the prophet [Micah 5:2]: 'But you, Bethlehem, in the land of Judah, are not the least among the rulers of Judah; for out of you shall come a Ruler who will shepherd My people Israel.' "

—Matthew 2:1–6

Note: The prophet Micah lived during the Babylonian captivity of the Jewish people approximately five hundred years before the Messiah would be born in Bethlehem.

Jack Kelley, in a Christmas study in gracethrufaith.com wrote that "the Magi were Parthian priests, descendants of the priesthood the prophet Daniel had organized in Persia some 500 years earlier. Parthia was a powerful kingdom north and east of Israel, a remnant of the Persian Empire that had recently defeated the Roman legions, and the Magi were among Parthia's most powerful leaders."[37]

The knowledge had been passed down through the generations. These Parthian priests knew from Daniel 9:24–27 the time of the arrival of the Messiah, and Micah 5:2 filled in where He would be born.

Bethlehem Was No Ordinary City

"A passage in the Mishnah indicates that the flocks that pastured in Bethlehem were raised exclusively to serve as sacrificial animals in the temple. The shepherds who watched over them were not ordinary shepherds. They were specifically trained for this task, hired and taught by the temple priests.

They were educated in what an animal that was to be sacrificed had to be, and it was their job to make sure that none of the animals were hurt, damaged, or blemished before sacrifice. In fact, when the ewe was ready to give birth, the shepherds would gently pull the baby lamb out and swaddle (wrap) it in cloths to help prevent it from injury and to keep it unblemished until its sacrifice.

The Mishnah forbade the keeping of flocks throughout the land of Israel, except in the wilderness. The only flocks otherwise kept so close to the villages were those for the temple services.

The males were for burnt offerings (sin); the female, for peace offerings. Thirty days before the Passover, whichever male animals were found fit for sacrifice were to be used for it."[38]

The Flight into Egypt

> Now when they had departed, behold, an angel of the Lord appeared to Joseph in a dream, saying, "Arise, take the young Child and His mother, flee to Egypt, and stay there until I bring you word; for Herod will seek the young Child to destroy Him."
>
> When he arose, he took the young Child and His mother by night and departed for Egypt, and was there until the death of Herod that it might be fulfilled which was spoken by the Lord through the prophet [Hosea 11:1], saying, "Out of Egypt I called My Son."

—Matthew 2:13–15

Murder of the Innocents

Distressed and infuriated by the thought of anyone challenging his throne, Herod issued a death sentence for the Messiah:

> Then Herod, when he saw that he was deceived by the wise men, was exceedingly angry; and he sent forth and put to death all the male children who were in Bethlehem and in all its districts, from two years old and under, according to the time which he had determined from the wise men. Then was fulfilled what was spoken by Jeremiah the prophet, saying:

"A voice was heard in Ramah,

Lamentation, weeping, and great mourning,

Rachel weeping for her children,

Refusing to be comforted,

Because they are no more."

—Matthew 2:16–18

The Death of Herod

Herod practiced Judaism, as did many Edomites and Nabateans who had intermarried with the Jews after they returned from captivity in Babylon. These Judaized Edomites were not considered Jewish by the Pharisees, though Herod likely considered himself a Jew.

In Acts 12:20–24 NIV, Herod displayed the ultimate Edomite trait, pride:

Then Herod went from Judea to Caesarea and stayed there. He had been quarreling with the people of Tyre and Sidon; they now joined together and sought an audience with him. After securing the support of Blastus, a trusted personal servant of the king, they asked for peace, because they depended on the king's country for their food supply.

On the appointed day Herod, wearing his royal robes, sat on his throne and delivered a public address to the people. They shouted, "This is the voice of a god, not of a man." Immediately, because Herod did not give praise to God, an angel of the Lord struck him down, and he was eaten by worms and died.

Herod distinguished himself from all other antichrist figures with the attempted murder of the Messiah Himself.

CHAPTER 8

NERO: ANTICHRIST #6

During his reign many abuses were severely punished
and put down, and no fewer new laws were made.
Punishment was inflicted on the Christians, a class of
men given to a new and mischievous superstition.

—Suetonius, Nero (XVI.2)

The Search for Amalek in Rome

In her book *The Esau Effect* (pp. 11-12) Kimberly
Rodgers writes:

A short history of Rome is necessary in order to continue piecing this together. The poet Virgil who lived
from 70 BC to 21 BC traced the founding of Rome to
King Latinus of Troy.

Rome's earliest history is shrouded in mystery. It was said to have been founded by the god Romulus in 753 BC. This is about 500 years after Latinus of Troy is said to have conquered it.

Historians have no plausible explanation for this discrepancy. The point is this: Rome was a city at least 500 years before Yeshua was born and perhaps for another 700 years prior to that. Rome is a VERY old city.

Going with the Latinus point of view, we can make sense of some of the traits of Rome. For instance, just the fact of the word Latin, which was the language of Rome for a very long time.

The Latins were a simple agrarian people that were hounded and infiltrated by the Greeks from the beginning. Sounds almost like an Edomite trait, doesn't it? This is important because Greek culture had the heaviest influence on the Latins, the Romans, of all the surrounding peoples.

Since it was Greece that conquered Troy, Latinus' home country, it makes sense that the Greeks followed Latinus to Rome and infiltrated the culture with Greek gods and the like, which is why Roman and Greek cultures are so much alike.

The hybridized Romans, seeking a national identity, later managed to give their gods different names than the names of the Greek gods, but the attributes of the Roman and Greek gods and cultures remained.

Both the Greeks and the Romans were conquering peoples. And when the armies needed more recruits, they hired them from outside their culture. Enter the Edomites, the descendants of Esau. Esau, who it was said would live by the sword! The ranks of the Roman Empire became filled with enlisted Edomites. Now these particular Edomites were not from the hybridized House of Judah. They were the original Edomites from the area of Mount Seir. Later, these Edomites would be an invading army against the House of Judah Edomites who defended Jerusalem.

But Edomites also got to the Roman Empire via another route. Edom came under the control of the Arabs in the 5th century BC. The mercenary Edomites among the Assyrians that moved north to Rome enlisted in large numbers into the Roman army. And often, if they did not volunteer for military service, they were conscripted.

One way or another, historians and rabbis alike agree that Rome and Edom became one and the same entity. First, the mingling of the darker, Semitic Edomites with the people of Italy account for the two distinct populations: darker, Semitic-like people in the south and fair skinned people in the north.[39]

The Beginning

Nero Claudius Caesar Augustus Germanicus (AD December 15, 37–June 9, 68) was Roman emperor from AD 54–68. This was the time in which Paul was carrying out his missionary journeys and the church was really starting to grow and take on a Gentile flavor. Nero was the sixth in the Julio-Claudian dynasty.

Nero was adopted by his great-uncle Claudius to become his heir and successor, and he succeeded to the throne in 54 following Claudius's death.

The Emperor Fiddles . . .

On the night of July 18, AD 64, a fire that began at the Circus Maximus burned nearly two-thirds of Rome. Many Romans believed Nero himself started it in order to clear land for his planned palatial complex, the Domus Aurea.

Tacitus, the Roman senator and historian, wrote:

It would not be easy to attempt an estimate of the private dwellings, tenement-blocks, and temples, which were lost; but the flames consumed, in their old-world sanctity, the great altar and chapel of the Arcadian Evander to the Present Hercules, the shrine of Jupiter Stator vowed by Romulus, the Palace of Numa, and the holy place of Vesta with the Penates of the Roman people.

To these must be added the precious trophies won upon so many fields, the glories of Greek art, and yet again the primitive and uncorrupted memorials of literary genius.[40]

Suetonius adds that every other interesting or memorable survival from the olden days went up in flames.[41]

Nero turned the blame for the fire onto the Jews because most of the Jewish section of the city was spared. In order to make his point, Nero began brutal persecution charging them with their supposed hatred of mankind.

Nero reigned over the empire and made an impact upon the early church and New Testament writings, such as, Romans 13 and 1 Peter 2, regarding submission to government, yet recognizing all authority is appointed by God. Nero was a political opportunist and an archenemy of the Jews.

The Roman historian Gaius Suetonius Tranquillus identifies Nero as a desperately wicked individual who grossly violated even basic civility through a long litany of disgusting demonstrations of depravity.

Nero's persecution knew no boundaries:

- He demanded to be worshiped as God (a common theme for antichrist figures).
- He dressed early Christians (Jews) in tar jackets, put them on stakes, and burned them at night to light his gardens.

- He ordered the brutal murders of some of his closest family members, including his mother Agrippina, and his wives Octavia and Poppaea.
- He had Poppaea's son, Rufrius Crispinius, drowned during a fishing trip for allegedly playing childhood games in which he pretended to be the emperor.
- He ordered the castration of a young boy named Sporus, whom he then married publicly.

Tacitus writes:

He castrated the boy Sporus and actually tried to make a woman of him; and he married him with all the usual ceremonies, including a dowry and a bridal veil, took him to his house attended by a great throng, and treated him as his wife. And the witty jest that someone made is still current, that it would have been well for the world if Nero's father Domitius had had that kind of wife.[42]

Suetonius places his account of the Nero-Sporus relationship in his reports of Nero's sexual aberrations between his raping a vestal virgin and committing incest with his mother. Some think that Nero used his marriage to Sporus to assuage the feelings of guilt he felt for kicking his pregnant wife Sabina to death. Dion Cassius, in a more detailed account, writes that Sporus bore an uncanny resemblance to (Poppaea) Sabina and that Nero called Sporus by her name.

In AD 68, prior to committing suicide during the siege of Jerusalem, Nero tried to stop the devastation after attributing a prophecy (Ezek. 25:14) to himself. He thought that even though God wanted the temple destroyed, He would punish the one who ordered it. That prophecy terrified Nero, and he converted to Judaism to avoid God's wrath.

Nero as Antichrist

After Nero's suicide in AD 68, there was a widespread belief, especially in the eastern provinces, that he was not dead and somehow would return. Suetonius relates how court astrologers had predicted Nero's fall but that he would have power in the East. And, indeed, at least three false claimants did present themselves as Nero redivivus [resurrected].[43]

From the apocalyptic pseudepigrapha (Jewish religious works circa 200 BC to AD 200, some of which were written by false authors) to the Sibylline Oracles (collection of apocalyptic Jewish and Christian verses, 200 BC to AD 200), Nero is depicted as Satan, who will come at the end of time as the incarnation of the dead Nero.

Augustine, in the fifth century AD, writing on 2 Thessalonians 2:7:

Some think that the Apostle Paul referred to the Roman empire, and that he was unwilling to use language more explicit, lest he should incur the calumnious charge of wishing ill to the empire which it was hoped would be eternal; so that in saying, "For the mystery of iniquity doth already work," he alluded to Nero, whose deeds already seemed to be as the deeds of Antichrist. And hence some suppose that he shall rise again and be Antichrist.

Others, again, suppose that he is not even dead, but that he was concealed that he might be supposed to have been killed, and that he now lives in concealment in the vigor of that same age which he had reached when he was believed to have perished, and will live until he is revealed in his own time and restored to his kingdom. But I wonder that men can be so audacious in their conjectures.[44]

What Is a Preterist?

Jack Kelley, at Gracethrufaith.com, says:

There's a group of scholars who believe that the Book of Revelation is all history and does not speak of the end times. They're called Preterists. Many of them don't believe in a Rapture, Great Tribulation, or Second Coming, but that only the judgment of mankind remains for future fulfillment.

They're correct in saying that each letter of the 22 letter Hebrew alphabet has a numerical value. There are no numbers in Hebrew so they used letters, and the numerical equivalent of Nero's full name and title

(Nero Caesar) in Hebrew (nrwn qsr) adds up to 666. So they claim that Nero is the antichrist that John was writing about.

The problem is that many other End Times prophecies were not fulfilled in the time of Nero, nor have they been since. Preterists twist the Scriptures to either deny those prophecies exist, or they find substitute fulfillment. For example, instead of having the antichrist stand in the Temple proclaiming he's God, the Abomination of Desolation, in 2 Thessalonians 2:4 and Daniel 9:27, they claim that when Rome affixed a large model of the Roman Eagle to the wall just outside the main gate of the Temple this prophecy was fulfilled.

Some Preterists also claim that the Second Coming prophecies were fulfilled on the Mount of Transfiguration when Jesus appeared in His glorified form to Peter, James, and John (Matt. 17:1–8).

There is no doubt that Nero was a model for the final antichrist, as were Antiochus Epiphanes before him and Hitler after him. But to make the claim that the prophecies of Revelation were all fulfilled during Nero's reign requires a gross departure from the literal, historical, grammatical interpretation of Scripture to which Futurists (those who believe the Revelation is about our future) adhere.[45]

Two Accounts: The Deaths of Peter and Paul

"In order to find out about the deaths of Peter and Paul, we have to look outside the New Testament. A number of letters and other literary works were written within the Christian community of the first century, but only twenty-seven made it into the New Testament. Books that did not make it into the New Testament are known as the *Apocrypha* (truthful accounts among fabricated stories, uninspired).

Among the New Testament Apocrypha is a book titled "The Acts of the Holy Apostles Peter and Paul," author unknown. In this book, we find a description of the deaths of Peter and Paul. Toward the end, we find Peter and Paul in front of Nero, and we pick up the story there:

Both Peter and Paul were led away from the presence of Nero. And Paul was beheaded on the Ostesian road. And Peter, having come to the cross, said: "Since my Lord Jesus Christ, who came down from the heaven upon the earth, was raised upon the cross upright, and He was deigned to call to heaven me, who am of the earth, my cross ought to be fixed head down most, so as to direct my feet towards heaven; for I am not worthy to be crucified like my Lord." Then having reversed the cross, they nailed his feet up."[46]

The second account is from first-century historian Josephus, who wrote that Nero was a barbarous individual who persecuted the church and Jews in Rome most severely (especially after the Great Fire) and was responsible for the deaths of the apostles Peter and Paul.[47]

CHAPTER 9

ADOLF HITLER: ANTICHRIST #7

Make the lie big, make it simple, keep saying it, and eventually they will believe it.

—Adolf Hitler

From the Belgian magazine *Knack* in 2010:

Jean-Paul Mulders, a Belgian journalist, and Marc Vermeeren, a historian, tracked down the Fuhrer's relatives, including an Austrian farmer who was his cousin, earlier this year. A chromosome called Haplogroup E1b1b1 which showed up in their samples is rare in Western Europe and is most commonly found in the Berbers of Morocco, Algeria and Tunisia, as well as among Ashkenazi and Sephardic Jews.

Haplogroup E1b1b1, which accounts for approximately 18 to 20 per cent of Ashkenazi and 8.6 per cent to 30 per cent of Sephardic Y-chromosomes, appears to be one of the major founding lineages of the Jewish population. Saliva samples taken from 39 relatives of the Nazi leader show he may have had biological links to the "subhuman" races (North Africa) that he tried to exterminate during the Holocaust. Hitler's concern over his descent was not unjustified. He was apparently not "pure" or "Aryan."

It is not the first time that historians have suggested Hitler had Jewish ancestry. His father, Alois, is thought to have been the illegitimate offspring of a maid called Maria Schicklgruber and a 19-year-old Jewish man called Frankenberger.

One can from this postulate that Hitler was related to people whom he despised.[48]

Hitler's Blood Gets Blood Boiling

A Google search on the subject of Hitler's illegitimate father's birth to an Austrian maid named Maria Schicklgruber will immediately show how this topic provokes historians, authors and conspiracy theorists on both sides of the issue.

In this chapter, we explore known facts and theories alike. While it is tempting to dismiss conspiracy theories as fiction, thousands of them, from Bernie Madoff to the Obamacare promises of keeping your healthcare plan, have proven true.

It can be argued that a theory is an alternative to the official mainstream storyline. In the new world order, separating the two is critical to gaining the truth.

Most writers reject the notion of Hitler having any trace of Jewish blood. This is despite the fact that upon conquering Austria in 1938, Hitler made his first priority to destroy the building containing his birth documents.

Hitler had always seen Austria as being part of Germany. He himself had been born in the Austrian town of Brannau, but for all his life, Hitler considered himself German.[49]

Hitler's obsession with hiding his bloodline makes the research even more compelling. Why would a leader of global power want to hide his birth records? Would not that leader want his legacy known?

An interesting parallel to this story is that for the first three years of the Obama administration, the US president did precisely the same thing. As Mark Twain said, "History doesn't repeat itself, but it does rhyme." Only after much secrecy and name-calling did a birth document for President Obama appear, seemingly out of nowhere. This is still a subject of much controversy today.

Was Hitler an Amalekite?

We know from the history of Esau's descendants that the Edomites moved into southern Israel during the sixth-century-BC Babylonian captivity when Israel was empty of Jews.

We also know that those same descendants of Esau intermarried with the returning Jews, creating a line that would produce the apostle Judas.

And we know that those same Edomite tribes moved northwest into Europe, dominating Roman and Greek cultures and flooding the continent with the covenant-breaking blood of Esau.

We can deduce, then, that the Fuhrer's obsession with exterminating an entire race of people, which he most certainly would have done had he succeeded in conquering the globe, was an identifiable trait of Amalek's self-loathing of his Jewish blood.

The possibility of Hitler having Jewish blood is still shrouded in controversy.

Hitler's Grandmother, Maria Schicklgruber

Maria was born on April 15, 1795 in an Austrian village. She was one of eleven children (only six survived) born to a poor rural family. Maria worked as a servant girl in wealthy Austrian homes, and here is where the story gets a bit complicated. There are two theories as to whom she worked for, so we will look at both.

Theory #1: Maria worked as a cook in the home of a wealthy Jewish family named Frankenberger. The speculation is that the nineteen-year-old Frankenberger son got Maria pregnant and regularly supported her after the birth of Adolf's father, Alois.[50]

Theory #2: That Maria worked in wealthy Jewish homes in Austria is not in dispute. However, in this version, the wealthy family was the famous Rothschild family. Maria was sent home to have her illegitimate child, who was born in Austria on January 7, 1837, with the name of Alois.

It is important to note that a child born out of wedlock in the nineteenth century was considered a major scandal and had to be dealt with quietly if no marriage was possible.

"Chancellor Dollfuss had ordered the Austrian police to conduct a thorough investigation into the Hitler family. As a result of this investigation a secret document was prepared which proved that Maria Anna Schicklgruber was living in Vienna at the time she conceived. At that time she was employed as a servant in the home of Baron Rothschild. As soon as the family discovered her pregnancy she was sent back to her home in Spital where Alois was born. If it is true that one of the Rothschilds is the real father of Alois Hitler, it would make Adolph a quarter Jew. According to these sources, Adolph Hitler knew of the existence of this document and the incriminating evidence it contained. In order to obtain it he precipitated events in Austria and initiated the assassination of Dollfuss. According to this story, he failed to obtain the document at that time, since Dollfuss had secreted it and, had told Schuschnigg of its whereabouts so that in the event of his death the independence of Austria would remain assured."[51]

The Rothschild family were formerly known as Bauers. The name *Rothschild* means "red shield," or *rotes-shild* in German, and was taken from the red shield, or hexagram/Star of David, on the front of their house in Frankfurt.

Remember that the color *red* is associated with Esau and the Edomite tribe.

Four Candidates for Alois's father

Candidate 1: Johann Georg Hiedler

Johann Georg moved in with Maria, her elderly father, and Alois (at age 5).

Many historians believe that Georg was the father of Alois, but they fail to explain why Alois maintained his illegitimate status, which made his life in the nineteenth century difficult.

The sole basis for this information dates to Alois's baptismal registry that shows Johann Georg claiming paternity over Alois on June 6, 1876, in front of three witnesses. At first glance, this seems like reliable information until you realize that Johann Georg would have been eighty-four years old and had actually died nineteen years earlier.[52]

Candidate 2: Johann Nepomuk Hiedler

At the age of ten, Alois was sent to live with Georg's brother, Johann Nepomuk, possibly because Maria was ill. She died a short time later.

Some historians believe that Nepomuk was the father. He helped raise Alois and left him a considerable inheritance.

The Hiedler brothers, however, are a poor fit to be Alois's father:

> Neither man claimed young Alois even though they had every opportunity to do so, even up to the time of Adolf's baptism. The baptismal record showed no known father.

Alois's mother went to her grave leaving the child to believe he was illegitimate.

Alois never questioned being illegitimate.

There are many versions of this story, but most point the finger at Johann Georg Hiedler's brother, Johann von Nepomuk Huetler. (The spelling of the last name was always changing—the baptismal registry spells it "Hitler.")

Some rumors say that because Johann von Nepomuk had no sons to carry on the name of Hitler, he decided to change Alois' name by claiming that his brother had told him that this was true. Since Alois had lived with Johann von Nepomuk for most of his childhood, it is believable that Alois seemed like his son. Other rumors actually claim that Johann von Nepomuk was Alois' real father and that in this way he could give his son his last name.

No matter who changed it, Alois Schicklgruber officially became Alois Hitler at thirty-nine years of age. Since Adolf was born after this name change, Adolf was born Adolf Hitler. But isn't it interesting how close it was? [53]

Candidate 3: Leopold Frankenberger, the Jewish Connection

In 1931, Adolf Hitler hired his attorney, Hans Frank, to find out once and for all if there was any truth to the Frankenberger rumor. Frank determined Maria did indeed work for a Jewish family named Frankenberger and that her child might have been conceived out of wedlock with the family's nineteen-year-old son.

From the book, *The Trial of the Germans*, by Eugene Davidson, University of Missouri Press, 1966:

"Frank undertook this delicate task, and he declared in the autobiography written in his cell at Nuremberg that what he discovered made it appear possible, if not likely, that Hitler's father had been half Jewish. The main facts are clear enough. Hitler's grandmother, a Fraulein Maria Anna Schicklgruber, worked as a cook for a well-to-do Jewish family named Frankenberger. The Frankenbergers had a son who was nineteen years old at the time Hitler's forty-two-year-old grandmother bore a child out of wedlock, and the Jewish family paid for the support of the child up to the time it was fourteen years old. Frank wrote that the money was given to avoid a public scandal. Apparently, although Frank does not say so, Fraeulein Schicklgruber had threatened to bring a suit against the Frankenbergers. Frank wrote that many letters were subsequently exchanged between them and Hitler's grandmother, which seemed to him to be evidence of a cordial relationship. Nevertheless, both he and Hitler were convinced that the child was actually the offspring of a millworker, Johann Georg Hiedler, a second cousin of Fraeulein Schicklgruber, who five years after the birth of the child married her and legitimized her son. But Frank, writing in Nuremberg no longer for the benefit of the Fuehrer, was also of the opinion that it was not out of the question that Hitler's father, who later changed his name from Hiedler to Hitler, was half Jewish."[53]

Hitler, unhappy with that report, ordered Rudolf Koppensteiner, a genealogist, to publish Hitler's family tree. Koppensteiner, despite angry protests from Hans Frank, was certain that the "illegitimate Alois Schicklgruber's father, who the mother later married . . ., was George Hiedler. Thus Hitler had an unblemished *Aryan* pedigree."[54]

From that time on, journalists scrambled as Hitler's pedigree became the hot topic for the people of Waldviertel (lower Austria). Hitler would have none of it, as he considered the matter closed with Koppensteiner's family tree.

Astonishingly, neither genealogists nor journalists picked up the obvious weak spot in Hitler's family tree, his father Alois Schicklgruber, who was born out of wedlock, whose father was uncertain.

Hitler did not want to hear anything about relatives: *I've got no idea about family history. In that area I'm an absolute dunce. Even when I was younger I didn't know I had relatives. I've only learned that since I became Reich chancellor. I am an entirely non-familial being, a non-clanning being by nature. That's not my cup of tea. I only belong to my folkish community.*

Not until after 1945 did Hitler's personal attorney, Hans Frank, former governor general in Poland, make truly explosive material public: shortly before he was executed he wrote in his memoirs—*Im Angesicht des Galgens (Facing the Gallows)*—where he mentioned the following bona fide scoop: at the end of 1930, he wrote, Hitler had shown him a letter, commenting that this was a disgusting blackmail story of one of the most repulsive relatives, concerning his, Hitler's, ancestry.

The relative had dropped off hints to the effect that in connection with certain remarks in the press one would be well advised not to broadcast certain circumstances of our family history.

The point was that Hitler had Jewish blood in his veins and therefore had scant credential for being anti-Semitic.[55]

The Frankenberger theory was later refuted by historian Ian Kershaw, claiming that all Jews had been expelled from the province of Styria (which includes Graz) in the fifteenth century and were not allowed to return until the 1860s. There is no evidence of a Frankenberger family living in Graz at that time.

Candidate 4: Baron Rothschild

1. Hitler's grandmother, Maria Anna Schicklgruber, a servant girl, came to Vienna and worked for wealthy families.

2. Maria became pregnant while working as a maid in the home of Baron Rothschild.

3. 1837: Maria was sent home, out of sight, where she gave birth to an illegitimate son named Alois, Hitler's father.

The Nizkor.org website contains Dr. Walter Langer's psychological analysis of Adolf Hitler commissioned by the Office of Strategic Services, Washington, D.C. An excerpt follows:

"Those who lend credence to this story point out several factors which seem to favor its plausibility:

... That the intelligence and behavior of Alois, as well as that of his two sons, is completely out of keeping with that usually found in Austrian peasant families. They point out that their ambitiousness and extraordinary political intuition is much more in harmony with the Rothschild tradition.

...That Alois Schicklgruber left his home village at an early age to seek his fortune in Vienna where his mother had worked

... That it would be peculiar for Alois Hitler, while working as a customs official in Braunau, should choose a Jew named Prinz, of Vienna, to act as Adolph's godfather unless he felt some kinship with the Jews himself."[56]

Alois Schicklgruber

Alois the boy learned to be an apprentice cobbler. At age eighteen, Alois joined the Frontier Guards, a semimilitary position and moved up to inspector of customs, but without further education, he could not advance. At age thirty-nine, Alois changed his name to Hiedler and was registered with the local church. The transfer of last names was inexplicably recorded as Hitler instead of Hiedler.[57]

1. 1873: Alois Schicklgruber married Anna Glass (no children).
2. 1876: Alois Schicklgruber's name changed to Hitler.
3. 1880: Alois divorced by his wife on grounds of adultery with Franziska Matzelsberger.
4. 1882: Franziska Matzelsberger bears Alois a son, also given the name of Alois.
5. 1883: Death of Alois's first wife; Alois marries Franziska Matzelsberger; Angela Hitler born.
6. 1884: Death of Alois' second wife, Franziska.
7. 1885: Alois's third marriage with Klara Pölzl, Hitler's mother.

Adolf Hitler Was Born in Austria, April 20, 1889

Hitler was born to Catholic parents. His father was reported to be lukewarm in his faith, but his mother was very devout. Hitler was confirmed in 1904 but did not often attend Mass.[58]

Although the subject of Hitler's possible Jewish heritage through the mystery of his illegitimate grandfather is the main topic of this study, it is equally important to understand how young Adolf's anti-Semitism began.

According to the Jewish Virtual Library:

The young Hitler was a resentful, discontented child. Moody, lazy, of unstable temperament, he was deeply hostile towards his strict, authoritarian father and strongly attached to his indulgent, hard-working mother, whose death from cancer in December 1908 was a shattering blow to the adolescent Hitler.

In Vienna he acquired his first education in politics by studying the demagogic techniques of the popular Christian-social Mayor, Karl Lueger, and picked up the stereotyped, obsessive anti-Semitism with its brutal, violent sexual connotations and concern with the "purity of blood" that remained with him to the end of his career.

In May 1913, Hitler left Vienna for Munich and when war broke out in August 1914, he joined the Sixteenth Bavarian Infantry Regiment, serving as a despatch runner. Hitler proved an able, courageous soldier, receiving the Iron Cross (First Class) for bravery, but did not rise above the rank of Lance Corporal.

Twice wounded, he was badly gassed four weeks before the end of the war and spent three months recuperating in a hospital in Pomerania.

Temporarily blinded and driven to impotent rage by the abortive November 1918 revolution in Germany as well as the military defeat, Hitler, once restored, was convinced that fate had chosen him to rescue a humiliated nation from the shackles of the Versailles Treaty, from Bolsheviks and Jews.[59]

Hitler Becomes a Leader

Hitler discovered a powerful talent for oratory as well as giving the new Party its symbol—the swastika—and its greeting "Heil."

His hoarse, grating voice, for all the bombastic, humorless, histrionic content of his speeches, dominated audiences by dint of his tone of impassioned conviction and gift for self-dramatization.

By November 1921, Hitler was recognized as Fuhrer of a movement which had 3,000 members, and boosted his personal power by organizing strong-arm squads to keep order at his meetings and break up those of his opponents. Out of these squads grew the storm troopers (SA) organized by Captain Ernst Röhm and Hitler's black-shirted personal bodyguard, the Schutzstaffel (SS).[60]

Hitler the Fuhrer

The destruction of the radical SA leadership under Ernst Rohm in the Blood Purge of June 1934 confirmed Hitler as undisputed dictator of the Third Reich and by the beginning of August, when he united the positions of Fuhrer and Chancellor on the death of von Hindenburg: he had all the powers of State in his hands.

Avoiding any institutionalization of authority and status which could challenge his own undisputed position as supreme arbiter, Hitler allowed subordinates like Himmler, Goering and Goebbels to mark out their own domains of arbitrary power while multiplying and duplicating offices to a bewildering degree.[61]

*http://en.wikipedia.org/wiki/File:Bundesarchiv_*
Bild_183-S33882,_Adolf_Hitler_retouched.jpg

Adolf Hitler Had Something to Hide

1. Maria Schicklgruber went to her grave leaving her child to believe he was illegitimate.

2. Alois Schicklgruber never questioned being illegitimate.

3. The Hiedler brothers are a poor fit to be Alois's father since neither man claimed young Alois even though they had many opportunities to do so.

4. Whether Hitler was a Frankenberger or Rothschild will never be known.

5. On Hitler's orders, the building containing his birth records was destroyed in 1938 when the German army conquered Austria.

6. Hitler's rejection of his possible Jewish heritage uncovered by Hans Frank.

Controversy is the hallmark of one of the most heinous mass-murderers in modern times. Hitler's total hatred and contempt for the Jews led him to want to erase the memory of the Jews from the earth, a common theme in the descendants of Esau. It is hard to imagine that Adolf Hitler will pale in comparison to the final Amalek.

CHAPTER 10

YASSER ARAFAT: ANTICHRIST #8

We plan to eliminate the state of Israel and establish a purely Palestinian state. We will make life unbearable for Jews by psychological warfare and population explosion. We Palestinians will take over everything, including all of Jerusalem.

—Yasser Arafat, 1996

To get a clear understanding of the origins of modern terrorism, it is necessary to explore the time line of the rebirth of Israel from 1917 to 1948. That Israel would be reborn in one day was prophesied in Isaiah 66:7–8 and fulfilled perfectly on May 14, 1948. Israel has been in a perpetual state of war ever since.

1917:

Britain signed the Balfour Declaration that committed Britain to establish a national home for the Jewish people.

1919:

World War I ended, the Ottoman Empire collapsed, and the Middle East was to be divided up.

1922:

1. League of Nations awarded Britain mandates over Transjordan, Palestine, and Iraq.
2. League of Nations awarded France mandates over Syria and Lebanon.
3. Britain awarded the entire land of Palestine to Israel with no territorial restrictions.
4. Israel was granted both sides of the Jordan River, totaling 43,075 square miles. A few months later, Britain, under pressure, altered the Balfour Declaration and took back 32,460 square miles, or 78 percent of the original land grant.
5. That land was then given to establish Transjordan, leaving Israel approximately 9,500 square miles.

1947:

1. The UN proposed a further reduction of land for Israel to 5,560 square miles, or 13 percent of the original land grant. Seventy-five percent of Israel's allotted land was desert.

2. Israel was pushed to land on the West Bank of the Jordan River.

3. Israel's land mass became 5,560 square miles; Arab land mass equaled 6,700,000 square miles.

4. The Arab world rejected the United Nations Partition Plan that would have created an Arab state and a Jewish state side by side.

1948:

1. The British Mandate terminated in mid-May.

2. Prior to Israel's statehood announcement, approximately 700,000 of 900,000 Arab refugees were warned of a pending war. The Arabs were advised to flee the area, for they might be mistaken for Israelis.

3. Iraqi Prime Minister Nuri Said declared, "We will smash the country with our guns and obliterate every place the Jews seek shelter in. The Arabs should conduct their wives and children to safe areas until the fighting has died down."[62]

4. Israel was born on May 14, 1948, and was attacked on the same day by Iraq, Jordan, Lebanon, and Syria. After the war, Egypt controlled the Gaza Strip and its more than 200,000 inhabitants but refused to allow the Palestinians into Egypt.

"Although demographic figures indicated that ample room for settlement existed in Syria, Damascus refused to consider accepting any refugees, except those who might refuse repatriation. Syria also declined to resettle 85,000 refugees in 1952–54, though it had been offered international funds to pay for the project.

Iraq was also expected to accept a large number of refugees, but proved unwilling. Lebanon insisted it had no room for the Palestinians. In 1950, the UN tried to resettle 150,000 refugees from Gaza in Libya, but was rebuffed by Egypt."[63]

Jordan was the only nation that allowed limited citizenship of Palestinian refugees. Approximately 40 percent of the 900,000 became citizens, but were put in refugee camps that developed from tented cities to rows of concrete blockhouses. The camps turned into urban ghettos. In 2004, concerned about increasing numbers of Palestinians in the country, Jordan began revoking citizenship from Palestinians who did not have the Israeli permits necessary to reside in the West Bank.[64]

5. Jerusalem was divided. Jordan occupied East Jerusalem and the West Bank.

1949: Armistice agreement was signed.

1967: The Six-Day War with Egypt, Jordan, and Syria was fought.

Israel captured the West Bank, East Jerusalem, the Gaza Strip, the Golan Heights, and the Sinai Peninsula. When Israel recaptured the West Bank from Jordan, King Abdullah *refused to repatriate* any more refugees and instead put them in internment camps.

It was in those camps, with the help of Yasser Arafat, that the name *Palestinian* became associated with Arabs from Jordan. Prior to 1967, Palestinian was a disparaging name for Jews living in Palestine (which was renamed Israel in 1948). Yet, since 1967, the UN has called these lands "occupied," even though the recaptured lands were part of the original British Mandate, and no nation has ever returned land taken during a defensive action.

The Right of Return

By the end of 2010, the number of Palestinian refugees on United Nations Relief and Workers Agency rolls had raised to nearly five million, several times the number that left Palestine in 1948.[65]

UNRWA's definition of a refugee also covers the descendants of persons who became refugees in 1948. The number of registered Palestine refugees (RPR) has subsequently grown from 914,000 in 1950 to approximately twelve million in 2013.

The *right of return* refers to the claims of first-generation Palestinian refugees and their descendants to recover the property they or their ancestors left after the 1919 collapse of the Ottoman Empire. These are the same refugees who turned down a two-state solution in 1947 and chose war instead.

In contrast with Israel's Jewish population of six million, the right of return of twelve million Palestinians would totally eliminate the Jewish majority and completely obliterate Israel as a Jewish state.

The Palestinian negotiators are clear that they will never accept peace without the right of return. Peace without *Jews* is the hidden agenda.

The Father of Modern-Day Terrorism

In August of 2004, Andrew McCarthy, in the *National Review*, wrote:

About him, while there is much to say, there is little to glean. He was a thug. One of the most cunning of all time for sure, but quite simply a ruthless, thoroughly corrupt, will-to-power thug.

As is often the case in the modern information age, just about everything in his life is known and almost nothing in his proffered legend is true. The man airbrushed in Thursday-morning encomiums from Kofi Annan and Jacques Chirac (among others) as the courageous symbol of Palestinian nationalism was not really named Yasser Arafat, was not a native Palestinian, and tended to sit out warfare with Israel whenever conventional fighting was involved.

Although he occasionally claimed to have hailed from what are now the Palestinian territories, Muhammad Abdel Rahman Abdel Rauf al-Qudwa al-Husseini was actually born in Egypt in 1929, the fifth child of a well-to-do merchant. He was educated in Cairo, although, after his mother's death when he was four, he lived at least part of the time with an uncle in Jerusalem.[66]

The Mainstream Press' Love Affair

Tom Gross, also writing for the *National Review*, in November 2004 summed up the mystery of the Left's love affair with Arafat:

Arab leaders long ago stopped liking or respecting Yasser Arafat, or indeed believing a word he said. Egyptian President Hosni Mubarak once referred to him, in the presence of Secretary of State Warren Christopher, as "a son of a dog." The Syrian defense minister called Arafat the "son of sixty-thousand whores."

Yet until the very end, some prominent Western journalists never stopped heaping praise on him, or covering up for his countless crimes and misdeeds. It didn't matter how many Jews, Arabs, and others died on his orders, or how many times he let down his own people, or stole from them. For these journalists, as well as for many European governments, he remained a worthy Nobel peace-prize winner and the "sole legitimate representative" of the Palestinian people.

To judge by some of the reporting as he lay on his deathbed in Paris—the hushed tone of the television newsreaders, the flattering touched-up portrait photos on the cover of the *London Times*—Arafat was a figure who deserved to be deeply revered, a kind of ailing pope.[67]

Arafat, the Early Years

Arafat was born August 24, 1929, in Cairo to Palestinian parents of means. It is important to note that Egypt did not grant citizenship to Palestinian refugees. It was in 2012 that Egypt began to grant limited citizenship to Palestinians, but only if the mother was Egyptian.[68]

Arafat lost his mother at the age of four, was educated in Cairo, but spent considerable time with an uncle in Jerusalem, which was still under British rule. The constant haggling over land between the Arabs and the returning Jews taught the young Arafat how to hate his Jewish neighbors.

While in college in Cairo, Arafat came under the influence of the Grand Mufti Haj Amin al-Husseini.

Husseini was the first proponent of militant, Arab Palestinian nationalism. He was an all or nothing terrorist who was determined to drive out or destroy the Jews or be destroyed himself, regardless of how many lives were wasted in the process.

Once he was in power, he began a campaign of terror and intimidation against anyone opposed to his rule and policies.

He not only killed Jews but also Arabs who did not support his campaign of violence. Husseini was not willing to negotiate or make any kind of compromise for the sake of peace.[69]

Britain was confused by the extreme hate and complete unwillingness of Husseini and made land concessions to the Arabs that reduced the original land grant from 43,065 square miles to 32,460 in 1922 (see timeline at beginning of chapter).

By 1948, the land grant had shrunk to 5,500 square miles, placing Britain in violation of God's covenant to Abraham, *"I will bless those who bless you and curse those who curse you."* The sun began to set on the British Empire.

Terror Timeline

In the mid-1950s, Arafat found work as an engineer in Kuwait. In 1957, he helped establish Fatah as a terror group dedicated to removing all Jewish influence in the Promised Land.

Fatah started out with soft targets like infrastructure and railroads but quickly moved on to attacking villages with the intent to inflict bloodshed and as much carnage as possible. Sound familiar?

In 1964, the Arab League created the Palestine Liberation Organization (PLO) as a tool in the war against Israel. Arafat's Fatah, which initially viewed the organization as a political opponent, gradually became the organization's dominant faction.

Following the humiliating defeat of the Arab forces in the 1967 War; the PLO decided that it could not rely on the Arab states to achieve its objective of destroying Israel. For the next ten years, this goal was the primary focus of the *massive terrorist campaign* by which the PLO's reputation was formed.[70]

Similar to terror groups of today, *the PLO's single purpose for its existence was, and still is, the destruction of Israel.*

Black September

In 1970, Arafat and an Arab-Palestinian force challenged King Hussein of Jordan by setting up a state within a state. That same year, in a foreshadowing of 9/11, the Palestinian army hijacked and blew up three airplanes that were flown into Jordan on September 12, 1970. The group became known as Black September and specialized in hijackings, resulting in the deaths of over two thousand passengers.

On December 28, 2007, the Egyptian magazine *Al-Ahram Al-Arabi* confirmed what many in the West had suspected for a long time: "that Yasser Arafat personally directed the Black September terrorist organization that claimed responsibility for the 1971 murder of Jordanian Prime Minister Wasfi at-Tal, the 1972 massacre of Israeli athletes at the Munich Olympics, and other atrocities."[71]

The Cairo newspaper quoted a book published in December 2007 by PLO leader Marwan Kanafani titled *Years of Hope*: "There have also long been claims that Arafat's longtime deputy

Mahmoud Abbas, who is still widely known in the Middle East by his military name Abu Mazen, was very closely involved in the Munich Olympics massacre."[72]

Both McCarthy and Gross describe Arafat as one of the most corrupt and ruthless murderers of all time. However, they do not realize the connection to the root of anti-Semitism stemming from the ancient bloodline of Esau, which makes him the almost perfect description of a twentieth-century Amalek.

Arafat, a distant descendant of Abraham, displayed a self-loathing of his Jewish blood that seemed to know no limit to the evil he was willing to inflict on the Jews.

Arafat's Criminal Enterprise

By the 1980s, Arafat had grown exceedingly wealthy. McCarthy continues:

> Though Arafat purported to have made it big in the engineering business in Kuwait, British investigators concluded after a searching probe, that his wealth stemmed from sidelines his organization maintained in "extortion, payoffs, illegal arms-dealing, drug trafficking, money laundering and fraud" that yielded billions.

> Throughout his career, moreover, Arafat proved a master at culling funds—whether from levies on strapped Palestinian workers or gushing subsidies from starry-eyed European and American governments. From these, he skimmed millions and stashed them

throughout the world—including in Israeli banks— keeping his wife on a lavish $100,000-per-month allowance in Paris while his people starved, and, of course, blamed Israel for their troubles.[73]

Arafat Ramps up Terror

February 21, 1970: Swissair flight 330 is blown out of the sky inbound to Tel Aviv. All passengers and crew lost.

May 8, 1970: Nine Israeli school children and three of their teachers are blown to bits when Arafat orders their school bus obliterated by bazooka fire.

September 5, 1972: Arafat's slaughter of eleven Israeli athletes at the Munich Olympics; Mahmoud Abbas is reported to have arranged financing for the operation.

March 1, 1973: The US ambassador to Sudan is among those killed when Arafat's thugs take over the Saudi embassy in Khartoum.

May 15, 1974: PLO terrorists toss grenades into a group of school children being held hostage in an elementary school in Ma'alot, Israel. Twenty-one children and two teachers are killed in the school.

The Achille Lauro

Throughout the 1980s, the Palestine Liberation Front (PLF), a terror group run by Mohamed Abbas and associated with the PLO, run by Yasser Arafat, conducted terror operations throughout the Middle East.

Abu (Mohammed) Abbas, not to be confused with Arafat's successor Mahmoud Abbas, aka Abu Mazen, was acting as PLF representative in the PLO's executive committee.

On October 7, 1985, four PLF terrorists boarded the *Achille Lauro* with the intent to hijack the vessel in exchange for fifty Arab-Palestinian prisoners being held in Israeli prisons. The four terrorists held the passengers hostage and directed the ship to Tartus, Syria.

Andrew McCarthy, *National Review*:

As his horrified wife looked on, the terrorists viciously shot a 69-year-old, wheelchair-bound Jew named Leon Klinghoffer, then tossed him overboard to die in the sea. Despite indications that the PLF was acting on instructions from PLO headquarters in Tunis, a State Department spokesman incredibly contended as late as 2002 that the PLF had been a renegade group broken off from the PFLP, and that Arafat was probably blameless in the Achille Lauro operation. But, aside from the fact that the PLO's website (for its UN mission) listed the PLF as one of its constituents, Abbas had actually been a member of Arafat's own PLO Executive Committee.[74]

Arafat Set Free

(Hosni) Mubarak allowed the PLF leader and hijacking mastermind, Mohammed Abbas, and the other terror-ists to fly to their headquarters in Tunisia. President

Ronald Reagan sent U.S. warplanes to intercept the flight, however, and forced it to land at a U.S.-Italian air base in Sicily. The United States and Italy fought over jurisdiction in the case, but the Italians refused to extradite any of the men.

Inexplicably, Abbas was allowed to go to Yugoslavia. An Italian court convicted 11 of 15 others associated with the hijacking, while Abbas and another terrorist were tried in absentia and found guilty. Abbas was sentenced to life in prison. Bassam al-Asker, one of the Achille Lauro hijackers, was granted parole in 1991. Ahmad Marrouf al-Assadi, another accomplice, disappeared in 1991 while on parole. Abbas was never arrested. In 1990, he struck again from the sea, with an abortive speedboat attack on bathers on a beach near Tel Aviv.

Though he was sentenced to five life terms in Italy, and was wanted in the United States, Abbas remained a free man. He spent most of the years after the hijacking in Tunisia before moving to the Gaza Strip in April 1996, after the Palestinian Authority took control of the area as part of the peace agreement with Israel.[75]

Mohammed Abbas died in 2004 in Iraq.

The First Intifada

On December 6, 1985, an Israeli citizen was stabbed to death while shopping in the Gaza Strip, which had been under Israeli control since the 1967 war. One day later, four Arab youths were killed in a car accident in Jabalya (northern Gaza).

Rumors spread that the accident was a revenge killing, and three days later an Arab youth was killed by an Israeli soldier after throwing a Molotov cocktail at an Israeli army patrol. The violence that erupted was led by Arafat's Fatah party. Joining in on the mayhem were the Popular Front, the Democratic Front, and the Palestine Communist Party.

After four years of violence, including 3,600 Molotov cocktails, one hundred hand grenades, and six hundred assaults, the death toll reached 1,100 Arabs, 1,400 Israeli citizens, and 1,700 Israeli soldiers.

The Madrid Conference

Hosted by the government of Spain, the three-day conference opened on October 30, 1991 shortly after the first Gulf War.

The four main participants of the conference were:

President George H. W. Bush

Secretary of State James Baker

Israeli Prime Minister Yitzhak Shamir

Head of the Arab/Palestinian delegation, Haydar Abd al-Shafi

The framework for peace consisted of three basic elements:

1. The *opening conference*—this called for the convening of an opening conference in order to inaugurate two separate yet parallel negotiating tracks.
2. The *bilateral track*—the bilateral negotiations were meant to resolve the conflicts of the past.
3. The *multilateral track*—the multilateral negotiations were meant to build the Middle East of the future while building confidence among the regional parties.[76]

Putting all the fancy tracks aside, the Madrid Conference was essentially a "land-for-peace" deal. Having turned down a two-state solution in 1947, the Arab side was demanding a state inside Israel without acknowledging Israel's right to exist.

In Genesis 12:3, God warned the nations that there would be blessings for those who blessed Israel and there would be curses for those who cursed her. Just to make His point doubly clear, God warned the nations that the land of Israel belonged to Him (Joel 3:1–2) and that it was not to be divided. Obviously, no one in Madrid that day knew or cared about God's word on the matter, and judgment was forthcoming.

As President George H. W. Bush was opening the Madrid Conference to consider "land for peace" and Israel's Middle East role, the "perfect storm" developed in the North Atlantic, creating the largest waves ever recorded in that region.

The storm traveled 1000 miles from "east to west" instead of the normal "west to east" pattern and crashed into the New England Coast. Thirty-five foot waves pounded Kennebunkport, Maine and destroyed the summer home of the Bush family.[77]

Madrid Outcome

The four leaders were elated at the end of the conference. The Israelis and Palestinians expressed their hope in the outcome.

Israeli Prime Minister Yitzhak Shamir: "With an open heart, we call on the Arab leaders to take the courageous step and respond to our outstretched hand in peace."

Head of the Palestinian delegation, Haydar Abd al-Shafi, November 1, 1991: "To the cosponsors and to the international community that seeks the achievement of a just peace in the Middle East; you have given us a fair hearing. You cared enough to listen and for that we thank you. Thank you."[78]

By 1993, with Bill Clinton winning the presidency, it became apparent that the agreements of the Madrid Conference were hopelessly bogged down.

Foolish men refused to acknowledge that peace in the Promised Land was impossible without God.

Arafat the Statesman

Despite the body count of both Jews and Arabs by the late 1980s to the early 1990s, Arafat was inexplicably granted observer status by the UN. This gave the terror group the right to participate, without the right to vote, in General Assembly meetings.

In an appeasement message to President George H. W. Bush, Arafat made the following statement: "As for terrorism . . . I repeat for the record that we totally and absolutely renounce all forms of terrorism, including individual, group and state terrorism."[79]

http://cache.20minutes.fr/img/photos/20mn/2012-07/2012-07-04/article_Arafat.jpg

In similar fashion, on November 30, 2012, the UN granted observer status to the successor of the PLO, Mahmoud Abbas's Palestinian Authority (PA). This was weeks after they launched rockets into Israel— confirming that thirty years of terror, bloodshed, and atrocities against the Jewish people *would be* tolerated and encouraged.

The fact that Arafat aligned with Saddam Hussein in the Iraq-Kuwait war while supporting the intifada almost sent him into obscurity. But Bill Clinton, sensing that Arafat was a key figure to Middle Eastern peace and a lasting legacy, gave the terror leader new life and made him a frequent visitor to the White House.

The Oslo Accords

The Oslo I agreement was an outgrowth of the Madrid Conference (land for peace) of 1991. The document was initially signed on August 13, 1993, when Arafat had his deputy Mahmoud Abbas sign for him, along with Shimon Peres of Israel and Warren Christopher of the United States.

Still unresolved were the Letters of Mutual Recognition resolving the PLO's rejection of violence and acknowledgment of Israel's right to exist. In exchange, Israel would recognize the unelected PLO as an official governing body and allow Arafat back into Judea (West Bank).

The parties then met secretly in a hotel in Paris. On September 13, 1993, the Accords were subsequently officially signed at a public ceremony in Washington, DC.

Attending were US president Bill Clinton, PLO chairman Yasser Arafat, and Israeli Prime Minister Yitzhak Rabin.

Once again, God's covenant to Abraham regarding the land was completely left out of the picture, and foolish leaders shook hands.

The Signers Face Consequences

On December 13, 1993, President Bill Clinton was faced with allegations that state troopers had arranged sexual relations for him while he was governor. One of the women mentioned was Paula Jones, a claim that persisted throughout his administration.

On November 4, 1995, Yitzhak Rabin was assassinated. The assassin, a religious Israeli named Yigal Amir, strenuously opposed Rabin's peace initiative of land for peace and particularly the signing of the Oslo Accords. Amir, a twenty-five-year-old Israeli resident of suburban Tel Aviv and law student at Bar-Ilan University, boarded a bus with a loaded gun and headed to a peace demonstration where one hundred thousand people had gathered to hear the prime minister and Labor leader Shimon Peres. Amir had planned to murder both Rabin and Peres for their roles in Oslo, but when Peres and Rabin walked off the podium separately after the rally, Rabin became the only target. He shot Rabin as the prime minister was entering his car.

Following this assassination, Shimon Peres, who had served in the Knesset and as prime minister, became the symbolic president of Israel, a position he still holds today at age ninety.

Yasser Arafat had his deputy and literal partner in crime, Mahmoud Abbas, sign the Oslo I document. Arafat referred to the Accords as the "peace of the brave," which is the same name that Mohammed gave to the Hudaybiyah Treaty that took place during the formation of Islam. It was a pivotal treaty between Mohammed, representing the state of Medina, and the Quraish tribe of Mecca in March AD 628. Mohammed never intended to keep the treaty and had his deputy sign on his behalf. Less than two years after making the treaty with the people of Mecca, Mohammed returned with an army, slaughtered the tribe, and took the city by surprise.

The Hudaybiyah Treaty lesson gave Arafat the model for Oslo. He would utilize the agreement to his benefit, have his deputy sign it, and then systematically violate every clause that did not suit his goal of the destruction of the Jewish state. Like Amalek's determination to be the first to draw Jewish blood, and Adolf Hitler's final solution, Arafat's plan was to eradicate the Jews completely.

Oslo Framework

Jack Kinsella (Omegaletter.com) wrote in his private briefing of September 28, 2003 titled *Mistake of the Century*:

> The Oslo agreement specifically took Jerusalem off the table. It forbade Yasser Arafat from assuming the title of "president" and made no provision for a Palestinian state.

> The Oslo framework called for a two-year period to follow in which Israel was to evaluate Palestinian success at limited self-rule, at which time, the territory administered by the PA would be expanded to several other Palestinian cities.

> If that was successful, the final stage of a set time frame of two years during which time, the Palestinians and Israelis (ostensibly now having been at peace for five years) would discuss the final status of Jerusalem. It was all supposed to be concluded by September 13, 2000, a period of exactly *seven years*.

> Within hours of the signing, Yasser Arafat stood on the Jericho-Jerusalem road and claimed it as part of

a new Palestinian state with Jerusalem as its capital. Oslo forbade any official Palestinian presence in Jerusalem. Arafat immediately set up his headquarters at Orient House in Jerusalem. Arafat also set up the curriculum for Palestinian schools, teaching that Israel stole the land from the Palestinians, produced maps of "Palestine" that made no provision for Israel, and taught a generation that the only way to achieve their goal of statehood was to kill as many Israelis as possible.

Like the current road map for peace, the only thing Oslo did was hamstring Israel. Arafat ignored any obligations that Oslo placed on him, rewrote the terms of Oslo in thin air, and found, to Israel's astonishment that the world was more than willing to believe Arafat's interpretation of the agreement, despite the fact the agreement itself still existed, and still bore Arafat's signature.

As a consequence, by the time Oslo was due to expire in September, 2000, Oslo was meaningless, and Arafat's 1993 pronouncement on the Jericho road was given legitimacy by *Ehud Barak, who offered Arafat all of the West Bank, all of the Gaza Strip and half of Jerusalem in exchange for peace.*(emphasis added)

Oslo II

The Oslo II Agreement, also known as the Taba Agreement, called for Israeli withdrawals from various Palestinian areas and expanded Palestinian self-rule. It divided the West Bank and Gaza into three areas: controlled by Israel, the Palestinians, or Palestinian civil authority with Israeli military control.

Oslo II also allowed a Palestinian election, which took place in 1996. Among other provisions, the agreement also provided "safe passage" to Palestinians traveling between Gaza and the West Bank, although Israel was also allowed to legally close crossing points into Israel if deemed necessary.[80]

A Future Oslo III: The Model for Daniel 9:27?

"Then he [antichrist] *shall confirm a covenant with many for one week; but in the middle of the week he shall bring an end to sacrifice and offering."*

The clue here is the word *confirm.* You cannot confirm something that does not already exist. Antichrist doesn't create a treaty, but enforces one already in existence. Daniel says that the treaty will be with "many" (Israel and neighbors), and "one week" in Hebrew (*shabua*) means seven years, making a modified Oslo III, a perfect fit for the future world leader.

The Second Al-Aqsa Intifada

From Ramallah, Arafat launched two intifadas in an effort to terrorize the Jewish people. Interestingly, the only state in the Middle East that has been willing to give the Arab Palestinians a state of their own is the Jewish state.

The second intifada began with prime minister Ariel Sharon's visit to the Al-Aqsa mosque on the Temple Mount in 2000, and the bloodshed continued until 2005. Arafat's motive to inflict as much cruelty as possible became apparent when his band of thugs turned their attention to murdering women and children. Like his predecessor Amalek, Arafat seemed to take pleasure in killing women and children.

Here are but two examples out of hundreds of documented atrocities:

On January 17, 2002, a Palestinian gunman burst into a bat mitzvah celebration in a banquet hall in Hadera, opening fire on the 180 guests with an M-16 assault rifle, killing six people and injuring thirty-five people. The Fatah Al-Aqsa Brigades claimed responsibility for the attack.

On May 27, 2002 a baby girl and her grandmother were killed when a suicide bomber detonated himself near an ice cream parlor outside a shopping mall in Petah Tikva, near Tel Aviv. The attack injured forty others, some seriously. Once again, Arafat's Al-Aqsa Martyrs' Brigades claimed responsibility for the attack.

In the time span of five years (2000-2005) the Arab-Palestinian death toll was 4,281 dead, of which 2,038 were civilians.

The Israeli death toll was 1,137 Israelis dead and 8,341 wounded. Of the wounded, 5,676 were civilians while 2,665 were security forces. The majority of casualties were caused by suicide bombers from the terror groups Hamas and Islamic Jihad.

Hamas and Islamic Jihad

To understand Hamas and Islamic Jihad, it is important to know their roots. While both terror groups have their origins in the Muslim Brotherhood, the book of Obadiah points these organizations directly from the bloodline of Esau: *"Because of the violence against your brother Jacob, you will be covered with shame; you will be destroyed forever"* (Obad. 1:10). Notice that Obadiah used the word *violence*, which in Hebrew is *chamas*. Chamas is pronounced "hamas." Rival terror groups emerged during the first intifada as offspring from the Muslim Brotherhood. Hamas's sole reason for existence is the destruction of the Jewish state.

The Nobel Prize

On December 10, 1994, in typical progressive Left fashion, the bloodthirsty Arafat was added to the 1994 Nobel Peace Prize, along with Shimon Peres (Israeli foreign minister) and Yitzhak Rabin (Israeli prime minister) for their efforts to create peace in the Middle East. Rabin's assassination on November 4, 1995 has given credence to Bible prophecy scholars who associate his assassination to be in fulfillment of God's promise to Abraham in Genesis 12:3.

This verse declares that those who injure God's people will not go unpunished, for he that touches the Israel of God shall be made to know that he touches the apple of His eye.

Ramallah: Arafat's Headquarters Point to Esau

Even Arafat's home base points to an Edomite connection. By the late 1990s, Arafat set up the PLO base of operations in the West Bank town of Ramallah.

In chapter 5, we discussed the sixth-century-BC movement of the Edomite tribe into southern Israel, including the lands of Judea (Idumea) and Samaria, known by the world today as the **West Bank**, a name disliked by the religious Israelis.

The returning Jews from Babylon intermarried with the descendants of Esau, wreaking havoc on the earth for the next 2,500 years.

How fitting that the father of modern-day terrorism would choose the West Bank area town of Ramallah to set up shop. His distant grandfather, Esau, would be proud.

The Death of a Terrorist

On November 11, 2004, Yasser Arafat died, and the baton was passed to Mahmoud Abbas.

According to DAFKA (.org), a consortium of students, faculty members, journalists, and concerned community activists, Arafat was well known by world leaders to be a vociferous homosexual pedophile.

In October 2000, J. R. Nyquist in an article in *World Net Daily* titled, "Kremlin Puppets and How They Work" wrote:

> Islam's strict moral code makes it easy for Russian intelligence services to penetrate Islamic countries and

recruit agents, because sin is not taken lightly in such countries. . . .

One chief example should serve to illustrate. In 1970 the Kremlin became interested in an obscure Arab construction engineer and collector of racecars, named Rahman al-Qudwa. Evidence shows, contrary to later claims, that this "construction engineer" was an Egyptian, born in Cairo during the summer of 1929. Rahman graduated from the University of Cairo and served as an officer in the Egyptian Army during the 1956 Suez campaign. Later he set up a business in Kuwait and made a fortune.

He then entered politics, founding a hopelessly small terrorist organization. But this terrorist organization would not remain hopelessly small forever.

According to the former head of Romanian intelligence, Lt. Gen. Ion Mihai Pacepa, who is one of the highest-ranking communist defectors of all time, Rahman al-Qudwa became an important political ally of the communist bloc following the death of Egypt's president, Gamal Abdul Nasser, in 1970. Gen. Pacepa's account of Rahman's intimate relations with the communist bloc is related in a book entitled *Red Horizons.*[81]

As it happens, Pacepa tells us that the Communists trusted Rahman because he was a voracious homosexual. This alone made him a workable Kremlin puppet, because once the Romanian intelligence services had taped Rahman's sex sessions with men and boys, he was completely in their hands. Afterwards, Rahman's friendship for the Communist bloc would be permanent—if he valued his growing popularity in the Arab world.

Rahman al-Qudwa is better known as Yasser Arafat, the chairman of the PLO since 1968 and the president of the Palestinian Authority—which is now at war with Israel. According to General Pacepa's account, Communist dictator Nicolae Ceausescu ordered his people to bring Arafat over to Romania. In late 1970, the chief of Romanian intelligence in Egypt, Gen. Constantine Munteanu, arrived in Bucharest with Arafat in tow. Munteanu had gathered an extensive file on Arafat, which characterized the PLO leader as "so much cleverness, blood, and filth all together in one man." Pacepa says that this was Munteanu's "standard definition of Arafat".

Since 2004, Arafat's cause of death has been attributed to:

- A stroke brought on by a mystery blood disorder
- A massive, hemorrhagic cerebrovascular accident
- The flu
- Poison by the Israelis

All are obvious distractions from the most likely diagnosis of AIDS.[82]

It is important to remember that homosexuals in the Muslim world are executed after likely being tortured. This induced

Arafat's supporters and worshipers to arrange a different out-come than AIDS for his demise.

Interestingly, Al-Kurdi, Arafat's personal physician for eighteen years, said "I would usually be summoned to attend to Arafat immediately, even when all he had was a simple cold. . . . But when his medical situation was really deteriorating, they chose not to call me at all."[83]

He also lamented that Arafat's widow, Suha, had refused an autopsy, which would have answered many questions regarding cause of death.

The latest theory began in 2010 with the dubious discovery of traces of polonium having been found, after six years, on the late terrorist's clothes. In order to both dispel rumors of AIDS as the cause of death and to blame the Israeli government at the same time, Arafat's body was exhumed in 2012.

On December 3, 2013 the UK news site BBC reported on the findings. As one would expect, the controversy intensified:

> A team of French scientists probing the death of Palestinian leader Yasser Arafat in 2004 do not believe he was poisoned, according to leaks from their report.
>
> They have reportedly concluded he died after a "generalised infection".
>
> A previous report by Swiss scientists said tests on his body showed "unexpected high activity" of polonium.

This "moderately" supported the theory, long believed by many Palestinians, that he was poisoned, the report said.

Arafat's widow, Suha Arafat, told reporters in Paris she was "upset by these contradictions by the best European experts on the matter...

In July 2012, an al-Jazeera documentary reported that scientists at the Swiss Institute of Radiation Physics had found "significant" traces of a highly radioactive and toxic material on personal effects given to Mr. Arafat's widow Suha after his death, including his trademark keffiyeh scarf.

Mrs. Arafat asked the Palestinian Authority to authorise the exhumation of his remains in order "to reveal the truth".

The Palestinian Authority granted French investigators and a team of Swiss scientists permission for the exhumation and to take samples for testing...

Last month [Nov. 2013], a forensic expert said that the levels of radioactive polonium found in Mr. Arafat's remains by the Swiss scientists were 18 to 36 times higher than normal.

In November, Palestinian officials said the third report, by Russian experts, did not give "sufficient evidence" to support the decision that Mr. Arafat was poisoned. However, experts who reviewed the document for al-Jazeera—which said it had obtained a copy—cast doubt on its findings."[84]

Chapter 11

SADDAM HUSSEIN: ANTICHRIST #9

"Three whom God should not have created: Persians, Jews, and flies."

So begins Saddam Hussein's pamphlet that was written by his uncle Khairallah Talfah, an Iraqi Ba'ath Party official. He wrote the ten-page pamphlet in 1940, and it was widely distributed throughout Iraq during the dictator's reign. The contents establish Saddam's hatred of the Jews.

Modern-Day Nebuchadnezzar

"This whole country will become a desolate wasteland, and these nations will serve the king of Babylon seventy years" (Jer. 25:11).

The Babylonian captivity began in 605 BC. King Nebuchadnezzar was fed up with Israel's King Jehoiakim for

161

plotting a rebellion against him. His second attack on Judah was in 597 BC, followed by the third in 586 BC.

God had instructed the Jews to allow the land to rest every seventh year. The Jews disobeyed God and did not give a Sabbath rest to the land. As God's judgment on them, in fulfillment of prophecies by Moses (Deut. 28:45–50), Isaiah (39:6), and Jeremiah (25:11), Nebuchadnezzar destroyed the temple and marched the Jews to Babylon.

Saddam himself believed that he was the reincarnation of King Nebuchadnezzar II and that he would usher in prosperity to his people and place the Jewish nation into slavery once again. The people of Iraq also believed he was the reincarnation of the ancient king Nebuchadnezzar. They trusted that Saddam Hussein possessed mystical, superhuman powers. They claimed he bioengineered giant scorpions, was tinkering with alien UFO technology, and had sheltered extraterrestrials.

The concept of a modern-day savior is hoped for in the Muslim world, as well as in the other two Abrahamic religions, Christianity and Judaism.

The Early Years

Saddam Hussein was born on April 27, 1937, in a village called a-Auja near Tikrit in northern Iraq. He never knew his father. It is said that he disappeared from Saddam's life.

Saddam's mother married a brutal man who was known to be both illiterate and immoral. *Saddam*, which means "crasher," an unusual name in Iraq, insisted on living with his uncle (his mother's brother, Khairallah Talfah) when he was released from prison in 1947. Saddam started primary school at the late age of ten and applied to the military at age eighteen. After failing to pass the entrance exam, which was a severe disappointment, he moved to Baghdad and attended high school, which he found boring.

Saddam's uncle was a member of the Ba'ath Party and introduced the young man to politics. Iraq had been under the British Mandate since World War I. Several political groups were vying for power. In 1957, at age twenty, Saddam joined the Ba'ath Party and was responsible for leading youth gangs in rioting. He quickly advanced and was put in charge of the assassination squad.

On October 7, 1959, he attempted to assassinate the prime minister of Iraq. Wanted and on the run, Saddam hid in Egypt for three years. While there, he attended law school at the University of Cairo. In 1963, the Ba'ath Party successfully overthrew the ruling Iraqi republic government and took power. This allowed Saddam to return to Iraq from exile. While home, he married his cousin, Sajida, the oldest daughter of Khairallah Talfah.

He was arrested in 1964 following a change in power but escaped from jail in 1967. In 1968, he helped lead the successful and nonviolent Ba'athist coup. He also gained a law degree from the University of Baghdad in 1968.

Tough Guy

Over the next decade, Saddam's power grew, and he became known as a thug. This description was also in keeping with the reputation of his hometown, Tikrit, which is still known as a rough part of the nation. On July 13, 1968, after the death of Iraq's president Abdel-Salam Aref, Saddam made a deal with the

Republican Guard. Hassan Al-Bakr became the president of Iraq, and Saddam "the Crasher" Hussein became deputy president. He insisted on being equal to the president and signing all official documents. It was two presidents for one, or as the people called it, "two-for-one."

Saddam, remembering his disappointment in being turned down by the military, insisted that Al-Bakr give him a general's ranking so that he could better manage the government. He was made a four-star general and given the red ribbon of a Staff College graduate.

Gen. Georges Sada, air marshal in the Iraqi Air Force, tells the story of Saddam's rise to the presidency. From his book *Saddam's Secrets*,

> ... [It was in] 1979 when Saddam finally told Al-Bakr that if he wanted to live, he would have to leave. Of course, Al-Bakr knew Saddam well enough by this time, so he left immediately.

> After Al-Bakr was gone... Saddam made himself president and only chose weak deputies to work for him. His purpose was to grow bigger while everyone else grew smaller and smaller. Before long he had made himself the absolute dictator of Iraq, and no one dared to resist him because they knew he was a ruthless killer.

> And this is how Saddam grew very large while the entire nation continued to shrink.[86]

Saddam, the Anti-Semite

It is no exaggeration to say that Saddam's hatred of Israel was of literal Biblical proportions. From the start of his regime, he pursued the grandiose goal of rebuilding the ancient Biblical city of Babylon. This fit with his thinking of being the modern incarnation of Nebuchadnezzar, the most important of the Chaldean or Neo-Babylonian kings, who ruled from 605 to 562 BC. In 597 and 586 Jerusalem was besieged and captured by Nebuchadnezzar; the second time, the king destroyed the city and carried the Jews off into their Babylonian captivity. Saddam hoped to do the same to the Jews of his day.

In Babylonia [Iraq], and most conspicuously in Babylon itself, Nebuchadnezzar engaged in numerous extravagant building projects. Picking up the mantle some 2,500 years later, Saddam embarked on a $200 million remake of the ancient city. In this re-erected Babylon, every tenth brick (among the sixty million) was inscribed, "Babylon was rebuilt in the reign of Saddam Hussein," as they had once carried Nebuchadnezzar's name.

Given these openly anti-Semitic ambitions, it was not exactly reassuring when Saddam in the early 1990s spoke publicly of "scorching half of Israel"—a country he called "an evil entity"—with chemical gas. Israelis feared that precisely that might be underway when, during the 1991 Gulf War, Saddam began firing Scud missiles at Tel Aviv. Israel had done nothing to provoke him, and in fact deliberately stayed out of the conflict out of fear of giving Saddam what he was seeking: an Israeli retaliation that would split the fragile Arab component of the Gulf War coalition. In a frightening reminder of the Holocaust, Israelis donned gas masks and placed their babies in special airtight cribs so they would not choke to death.

Saddam never gave up his hatred of Jews, nor his love of terrorism: In April 2002—almost exactly one year before he would flee from American tanks—Saddam publicly upped the payment from $10,000 to $25,000 for the families of Palestinian suicide bombers who blew themselves up in the service of killing Israel's Jews.[87]

Without public announcement or debate, the authorities in Iraq ordered the reconstruction of one of the most audacious symbols in Baghdad of Saddam's long, violent and oppressive rule: the Victory Arch, two enormous sets of crossed swords, clutched in hands modeled after his very own.[88]

The swords are an eerie reminder of Genesis 27:40 *"By your sword you shall live, and you shall serve your brother,"* the words spoken in the blessing that Esau demanded from his father Isaac.

About Chemical Weapons

As early as April 1987, the Iraqis used chemical weapons to remove Kurds from their villages in northern Iraq during the Anfal campaign. It is estimated that chemical weapons were used on approximately 40 Kurdish villages, with the largest of these attacks occurring on March 16, 1988 against the Kurdish town of Halabja.

Beginning in the morning on March 16, 1988 and continuing all night, the Iraqis rained down volley after volley of bombs filled with a deadly mixture of mustard gas and nerve agents on Halabja. Immediate effects of the chemicals included blindness, vomiting, blisters, convulsions, and asphyxiation. Approximately 5,000 women, men, and children died within days of the attacks. Long-term effects included permanent blindness, cancer, and birth defects. An estimated 10,000 lived, but live daily with the disfigurement and sicknesses from the chemical weapons.

Saddam Hussein's cousin, Ali Hassan al-Majid, was directly in charge of the chemical attacks against the Kurds, earning him the epithet, "Chemical Ali."[89]

In February of 1998, Madeleine Albright said, "Iraq is a long way from [here], but what happens there matters a great deal here. For the risks that the leaders of a rogue state will use—nuclear, chemical, or biological weapons—against us or our allies is the greatest threat we face."[90]

From Gen. Georges Sada's book:

Everybody understood that reality at the start of the [Iraq] war. I'm convinced it was only politics that made some people change their minds about the facts. Iraqi engineers are very good at manufacturing chemical weapons systems for artillery shells, rockets, missiles, and other ordinance... the chemical and mechanical engineers continued building and developing all these systems, on into 2003 and after the American invasion began.

The point is that... he knew he would have to take special measures to destroy, hide, or at least disguise his stashes of biological and chemical weapons, along with his laboratories, equipment, and plans associated with nuclear weapons development. But then much to his good fortune, a natural disaster occurring in neighboring Syria provided the perfect cover story for moving a large number of those things out of the country.

Furthermore, I know the names of those who were involved in smuggling WMDs out of Iraq in 2002 and 2003. I know the names of the officers of the front company, SES, who received the weapons from

Saddam. I know how and when they were transported and shipped out of Iraq.[86]

It was through the use of WMD that Saddam planned to intimidate and control the Middle East. Saddam planned to follow through on his motto *Control Middle East oil, Control the world.*

In 1990, Saddam was talked out of a planned full-scale invasion of Israel. General Sada, risking his life, was able to convince Saddam that Israel's military systems were far superior to the antiquated Iraqi systems. General Sada metaphorically explained that Iraqi radar technology in comparison to the Israeli system would be like the difference *between men who are blind and men who can see.*

But once Saddam had the necessary WMD to control Middle Eastern oil and hold the West hostage, he would make good on his plan to finish what Nebuchadnezzar started. Saddam would finish off the Jews and finally carry out his ancient predecessor Esau's wish to kill his brother Jacob (Gen. 27:41).

http://en.wikipedia.org/ wiki/File:Saddam_Hussein_at_trial,_July_2004-edit1.jpeg

Saddam Is Hanged

Christians believe that God ordains events, and that "coincidence" is a word the secular world uses to explain supernatural occurrences. The comparisons between Saddam's hanging and the Jewish feast of Purim (see chapter 5) are enough to fill another chapter.

For the sake of brevity, we have the following outline:

1. Haman was descended from Agag, the king of the Amalekites. Agag was overthrown by King Saul (1 Samuel 15; Est. 3:1).

2. Amalekites and Agagites are direct descendants of Esau's tribe, the Edomites. Saul failed to follow God's instructions to kill all the Agagites when he spared King Agag's life.

3. The Jewish feast of Purim in the book of Esther celebrates the victory of the Jews over the Persian Amalekite Haman.

4. Saddam Hussein was captured on December 13, 2003, when he was pulled out of the so-called "spider hole" just south of Tikrit, his hometown. This date is a type of Purim, because it was the thirteenth day of the twelfth month on our calendar, while Purim is the thirteenth day of the twelfth month on the Hebrew calendar (Est. 9:17).

5. The first Gulf War ended on the first day of Purim, and the second Gulf War began on the second day of Purim.

6. After the victory of the Jews over the Persians, Haman was hanged on his own gallows, as was Saddam.

7. Finally, Nebuchadnezzar ruled from Babylon. In 1982, Saddam's workers began reconstructing Babylon's most imposing building, the six-hundred-room palace of King Nebuchadnezzar II.

For Such a Time as This

God always provides a protector *"for such a time as this"* (Est. 4:14). In Jacob's blessing in Genesis 27:29, we are reminded that no tyrant will succeed—*"May nations serve you and peoples bow down to you"*— and at the millennial reign of Jesus Christ, the nations will indeed bow to Israel.

CHAPTER 12

THE DISAPPEARANCES: ANTICHRIST #10

The following is a fictional scenario of the rapture of the church and the emergence of the final antichrist.

President Obama, nearing the end of eight tumultuous years, was ready for a new job, and as fate would have it, one was about to be offered to him.

Ban Ki Moon, Secretary-General of the United Nations, was ready to announce his retirement to be effective at the end of his term on December 31, 2016. The world was ready for new leadership, and Ban, nearing seventy-two, was exhausted.

The UN vacancy, if accepted, would be a perfect fit for the internationally popular US president.

By the end of summer 2016, the upcoming US elections were in full swing. The US electorate was stunned by Hillary Clinton's sudden withdrawal, and speculation centered on a neurological disorder first diagnosed after the Benghazi massacre of 2012.

A few days after Labor Day, Janet Napolitano threw her hat in the ring for president of the United States. The nation was more than ready for a woman candidate, and Napolitano's soft stance on terrorism and experience at Homeland Security fit well with the Democrat Party leaders. The often-heard reports of her personal relationships made her even more popular, and Joe Biden lagged far behind in the number-two slot.

Wars and Rumors of War

As the Jews in Israel gathered for Sukkot, a missile barrage originated from the south in Gaza, reminiscent of the Thanksgiving attack of 2012. On that Thanksgiving weekend, rockets had landed close to Jerusalem, and for the first time since the 1990s, sirens had sounded in Tel Aviv.

But this attack was different. This time a coalition of seven Arab nations coordinated the assault with the intention to end the Jewish presence in Israel for good. The three-thousand-year-old prophecy of Psalm 83 was in high gear.

Missiles were coming in with deadly accuracy, and several targets were hit in Tel Aviv, inflicting extensive damage to government buildings, with heavy casualties being reported.

At the same time, Hezbollah activated a large-scale rocket assault from the north in Lebanon, which overwhelmed Israel's Iron Dome missile-defense system. With no choices left, the Israeli air force launched F-161 Sufa fighter jets armed with nuclear-tipped cruise missiles.

Egypt and its armies in the Sinai, as well as the Saudis and al Qaeda forces from northern Iraq, were the first to surrender as

Israeli Defense Forces (IDF) struck with a swift missile launch that decapitated those nations' governments.

Jordan had been teetering on the brink of financial collapse; nevertheless, King Abdullah made the decision to join the Arab attack on Israel, only to be crushed as well.

But it was Syria that took the worst hit. After the Assad government attempted a desperate chemical-weapons attack on Tel Aviv, the IDF unleashed an overwhelming nuclear attack on Damascus from the Israeli Dolphin submarines that had been patrolling offshore. Known as the world's oldest continuously inhabited city, Damascus and its two million residents were gone overnight, fulfilling the 2,700-year-old prophecy of Isaiah 17:14.

The seven Arab nations suffered widespread damage from the war. Muslim leaders were largely silent after their crushing defeat, and the Palestinian Authority, under its illegitimate president Mahmoud Abbas, was wiped out.

Terror groups like Hezbollah and Hamas sustained mass casualties, resulting in the loss of their leaders. The Israeli Defense Force was so effective that Israel was said to have been miraculously aided.

The Edomite armies of Psalm 83 were gone, precisely as Obadiah 1:18 had prophesied more than 2,500 years earlier. Now Israel was being pressured into signing a treaty with its decimated neighbors.

Israel was again in control of the West Bank, Gaza, and East Jerusalem. Tight security, from the Sinai in the south to the Golan Heights in the north, was immediately established.

Day 1: The Disappearances

It happened in a flash, in the twinkling of an eye, a sudden phenomenon that led to economic collapse and complete global chaos. The instantaneous disappearance of just over 1 billion people eclipsed the massive Middle East war that had recently destroyed Damascus, and abruptly diverted the world's attention.

Absolutely no one on earth had been able to predict with any certainty the timing of Jesus' promise to come for His church. No man knew the day or hour, as prophesied in Matthew 24:36.

Babies sleeping in their cribs—gone in a moment. Mothers making supper for their families—vanished. Children playing in the backyard—nowhere to be found. Grief-stricken parents stared at empty beds, strollers, and car seats. Rumors of spaceships and alien kidnappings were rampant.

Cars were crashing on highways with no drivers at the wheel; airlines were reporting panic as numerous passengers and crews vanished midflight. As minutes turned to hours, a full-scale alarm was under way. Cell-phone networks were overwhelmed, as were the phone lines. When the Internet kill-switch was activated by world governments, people ran from their houses, seeking terrified neighbors for any news.

Hardest hit was the United States of America with its reported 73 percent Christian population. It would take months to get an accurate count of those who were missing, since the leadership of the nation was in shambles. Thousands of pastors, priests, and church leaders from every denomination were no longer around to explain what had happened.

Many "Christian" leaders went on government-regulated television to explain that this had nothing to do with God and that NASA experts on extraterrestrial phenomena were suspecting a mass-kidnapping occurrence.

Reverend Bill Peterson of the Anglican Church, Bishop Barbara Tingsley of the United Methodist Church, Roman Catholic Archbishop Jack Riley of New York, and Rabbi Harold Kirchbaum of Baltimore assembled that night in a CNN special report intended to shed light on what had happened.

The panel, in soothing voices, using isolated Bible verses as proof, attempted to disprove the notion that Jesus had returned for His church. The group explained that the teaching of a "rapture event" was a misinterpretation of Scripture and that all of Bible prophecy and the book of Revelation had been fulfilled at the destruction of the second Jewish Temple in AD 70. Antichrist, they said, was the Roman emperor Nero.

The world was desperate for answers. The public, having little or no Bible knowledge, seemed to accept the clerics' every word, as over one hundred million viewers tuned in to the program.

As the search for missing loved ones led to one dead-end after another, terrified people the world over began to rehash the years prior to the disappearances to try to figure out an explanation.

Had there been signs that were missed or overlooked? Had the people of the world drifted so far from the Bible that the writings of the prophets had been discarded as fables or stories?

One man would soon stand up to calm a panicked world.

Day 2: Emergency Meetings

President Obama held an emergency cabinet meeting at 11:00 a.m. The first order of business was to try to explain the disappearances and attempt to restore calm to the nation.

Before anyone could speak, National Security advisor Susan Rice stood up. She announced that the president was ready to implement a change to the security of the United States.

Rice, in uncharacteristically forceful tones, informed the cabinet that in light of the mysterious events of the past day, the president was ready to put into operation a new security plan for the United States, one that had been in the planning stages for years.

"The president," Rice explained, "is going on live TV at 8:00 p.m. Eastern Standard Time to announce that the Department of Homeland Security will be changed, under a provision of the 2010 Affordable Care Act law, to the National Civilian Force" (NCF).

The president's decision was a reminder to the members of the cabinet of a speech he had made while still an Illinois senator in 2008. In it, he had said, "We cannot continue to rely on our military in order to achieve the national-security objectives that we've set. *We've got to have a civilian national-security force that's just as powerful, just as strong, just as well-funded.*"

The president, still seated, thanked Secretary Rice for her remarks. As he rose to his feet, an unusually angry attitude was obvious. President Obama reminded those assembled that the responsibility to protect the American people and to restore order was on his shoulders. As commander-in-chief, he was required to take bold and decisive steps. Looking directly at a stunned

Speaker of the House, the president said, "These actions are the right thing to do, and there will be no more discussion about it."

He motioned to Rice, and she continued. "Beginning in 2010 and through 2013, Homeland Security chief Janet Napolitano had been authorized to build a fleet of more than 10,000 armed drone aircraft, 15,000 domestic tanks, and a stockpile of more than two billion rounds of ammunition."

The hollow-point bullet orders had stunned the blogosphere in 2012 but were ignored by the mainstream press.

"The civilian army, the National Civilian Force, will be armed and dangerous," Rice said. "Security will be tightened until answers become clear as to how the disappearances happened. The administration will not rest until the perpetrators are found and held accountable."

Rice specified that armed drones would fill the skies of America in similar manner to the armed soldiers in the nation's airports after 9/11.

In addition, the president would retain all decision-making power and fully use the controls granted to him by Congress under the National Defense Authorization Act of 2013. The NDAA authorized the president to arrest and detain indefinitely any suspicious US citizen, without cause. The now-empty prison at Guantanamo Bay, Cuba, would be utilized for incarceration. It was the perfect venue, far away from the press and from captives' family members.

Rice explained that the NCF would be expanded from the 240,000 current employees to over 400,000, including civilians and select military personnel that had returned from Afghanistan.

Her final words at the meeting were, "The president, without delay, will enact the National Defense Resource Preparedness Act to officially declare martial law, effective immediately."

Day 3: An Assault on the Dollar

An economic meeting convened with top administration officials, including former Obama economic advisor Larry Summers, Federal Reserve chairman Janet Yellen, and CIA head John Brennan. This special session was chaired by the current Treasury secretary, Jack Lew.

As the top-secret meeting got under way, John Brennan had disturbing news to share. He informed the group that there was urgent intel from our people on the ground in the Far East. China was about to make a move with support from Japan, Russia, and the European Union to dump the dollar as the world reserve currency. They planned to institute the renminbi, either alone or as part of a basket of currencies called Special Drawing Rights (SDRs), which would include the euro and the yen.

Brennan told the cabinet that China had been buying large amounts of gold for the past five years in an effort to build global confidence in the Chinese currency. Their aim was to make the renminbi the de facto reserve currency and to increase global influence.

China had been building support from Australia and Brazil since 2013 by enacting currency swaps to enable the direct convertibility of their currencies into Chinese renminbi, without US dollar intermediation.

Day 4: The United Nations

Ban Ki Moon and the other leaders from the Quartet (United States, United Nations, European Union, and Russia) met in a closed-door emergency meeting in New York.

Ban had called the Quartet together for discussions on the Middle Eastern peace deal. They agreed that it was imperative to convince Prime Minister Netanyahu that unless he wanted the wrath of the whole world to come down on Israel, the peace deal, which was still unsigned, was in Israel's best interests. No one cared that the Arab nations had started the war. They knew the prime minister would have to give in.

President Obama then informed the group that the Chinese government was about to attempt to dethrone the dollar as the world reserve currency. This move would make everyone forget that one billion people had vanished. If nothing was done to stop the Chinese, the US dollar would crash.

On that day, only professional traders were interested in the markets, and only marginally at that; people all over the world were more interested in answers about missing loved ones. The stock-market ticker was barely moving.

At 2:00 p.m., rumors of a poorly bid Treasury auction of ten-year bonds started to rattle the bond market. Reports had been circulating for years that China and Japan had been curbing their purchases of US Treasury bonds because of unrestrained spending by the US government.

Day 5: The Federal Reserve

The US auctioned off longer-term Treasury bonds with even worse results, indicating that US debt was no longer attractive at current interest-rate levels.

In an attempt to calm financial markets, Federal Reserve chairman Janet Yellen appeared before the Senate Banking Committee to explain why Quantitative Easing (QE) 4, the same money-creation scheme that had seemed to work for her predecessor, was having little or no effect on the recent market sell-off.

The conversation shifted instead to the weak bond auctions of the past two days.

Committee chairman Mike Reed (R, Florida) reminded those present that if other nations such as China, Japan, or Russia were unwilling to finance the country's two-trillion-dollar deficit and the national debt of almost twenty trillion dollars, interest rates would necessarily rise quickly and destroy the fragile housing market.

Chairman Yellen was a reassuring presence that morning, explaining to Congress that there was nothing to worry about as far as America's ability to continue to borrow. She said the Fed had its finger on the pulse of the economy and was prepared to buy up all the bonds that had not been bid for in the recent Treasury auctions. Yellen's comments, however, had little effect in calming the markets.

Traders on global exchanges knew that Yellen's comments meant that the Fed would simply "create" more money to finance America's exploding debt. By noon, the Dow Jones Industrial Index was down by almost 1,100 points.

As the rumors of a spike in interest rates spread, Goldman Sachs's chief of fixed-income securities tried to reassure Goldman's high net-worth clients that the party wasn't over until the Fed stopped providing stimulus to the economy. Friday's market rallied before the 4:00 p.m. close as bargain hunters entered the market, and the Dow Jones Industrial closed down 397 points to 12,797.

Day 6: China Makes a Move

The New York Stock Exchange opened down 452 points as traders focused on the events of the prior week, but the big news was in the precious-metals market. Gold traded up 84 dollars to a new high at 2,818 dollars per ounce, and silver topped 63 dollars per ounce. Traders attributed the rise in precious metals to more money printing by central banks, yet that was just the tip of the iceberg.

At 10:00 a.m. New York time, China announced an expansion of its 2013 currency swaps with Australia and Brazil that would now also extend to the EU, Japan, India, and Russia.

The transactions were meant to bypass the US dollar in purchasing global commodities and to bring in the Chinese renminbi as the new world reserve currency. The G8 was fed up with a lack of US fiscal discipline, and with oil at 150 dollars per barrel, something had to be done.

Global equity markets cratered again as gold rallied past three thousand dollars. Startled nations began selling Treasury bonds, driving up interest rates.

By 2:00 p.m., the ten-year benchmark Treasury yield was 5.9 percent up—almost three hundred basis points from the previous night's close.

China was ready to roll the dice on 1.2 trillion dollars in US Treasuries in order to make the renminbi the new world reserve currency.

Geopolitical Alliances

The European Union was still reeling from the enormous debt of its southern countries. The stronger, northern EU nations summoned emergency meetings to shore up much-needed capital, as cash reserves, even in Germany, were dangerously low.

By early 2015, it was evident that the European Union was in dire straits as Greece, Portugal, Italy, and Spain were once again about to default on sovereign debt. Since Western nations were no longer willing to contribute to a dying cause, new capital was available only from the European Central Bank's (ECB) printing press.

By late 2015, it had become clear that the European Union's twenty-eight nations might break apart. The ECB's bailout only weakened the euro further, worsening the situation as the price of goods and services skyrocketed.

Merger talks that had been stalled between the European Union and the Union for the Mediterranean (UfM) since 2013 were once again on the table.

The UfM-EU partnership would bring the number of nations in the federation to sixty-nine. Israel and the Arab states that had been defeated in the recent Arab-Israeli war were forced by the pending Middle East peace accord to join the new alliance.

Only one more nation was needed for the UfM to acquire the same global footprint as the ancient Roman Empire. The Arab-Israeli war had forced independent nations to a geopolitical game of *musical chairs*.

Turkey Aligns with Russia

Turkey moved to ditch NATO and its UfM membership by applying to join the Shanghai Cooperation Organization (SCO).

Founded in 2001, the Beijing-based SCO consisted of Russia, China, Kazakhstan, Kyrgyzstan, Tajikistan, and Uzbekistan. Afghanistan, India, Iran, Mongolia, and Pakistan had observer status in the political and military organization.

In 2013, Turkey had emerged as a Middle Eastern power-house. Having been turned down from joining the European Union in 2012, the Muslim nation had a score to settle, and joining Russia and China would fit the bill.

Turkey's economy was thriving. In recent years, Turkey's private sector had been rapidly growing, and with a 6.7 percent average GDP for the past three years, the Islamist state played a major role in industry, banking, and communications.

But of major importance to Russia and China, after the global turmoil of the Middle Eastern war and the disappearances, was the fact that Turkey had built one of the largest and most powerful militaries in the world.

Ukraine Breaks Apart

In December 2013, masked protestors in Kiev had attached steel ropes to the monument of Vladimir Lenin, pulled it down, and reminiscent of Saddam Hussein's statue—smashed the granite figure with sledgehammers. The activists shouted, "[President Viktor] Yanukovich, you'll be next!"

Ukraine is a very old country, having been part of the Assyrian Empire that dominated the known world in three stages from 2500 to 700 BC. Between 700 and 200 BC, Ukraine was part of the Scythian kingdom. It was the area known for first domesticating the horse.

http://en.wikipedia.org/wiki/File:Grody_czerwienskie.png

Descendants of Esau had migrated from Judea and Persia (Iran) north into Turkey, where they were called Chazars. From there, they spread into Ukraine and Russia, where they were known as the fierce Scythian tribe of horsemen renowned for deadly accuracy with a bow and arrow while riding at full gallop. Later, the Roman Empire under Hadrian (AD 117–138) was in control of the western part of Ukraine.

West Ukraine became known as *Red Ruthenia* in Medieval times. The association of the color red with Esau and Edom is not lost in the comparison with Ukraine.

The new West Ukraine applied for UfM membership and was on the fast track for approval. Their inclusion would bring the number of nations to seventy. The rider on the white horse (Scythian symbolism) of Revelation 6:2 and the revived Roman Empire of Daniel 7:23 were clearly in focus.

Day 7: Ten Regions

Because of the tremendous size and diverse ethnicity of the new UfM, an emergency mandate was implemented to divide the soon-to-be seventy nations into ten geographical regions, fulfilling Daniel 7:24, and to appoint a head for each one. Next, an election by the leaders of the governing nations selected a surprise representative to the UN.

The UfM appointed Antonio Volodymyr, a young, handsome political newcomer from Ukraine, to head the UN delegation, while the Ukraine application's approval was being signed.

Volodymyr, who had been educated in England, was possibly the greatest orator since Barack Obama first burst onto the world stage in 2004. His Italian-Jewish mother and Ukrainian-Moslem father, combined with his total mastery of five languages, made him the man of the hour. He was ideally suited to the new world order.

The Arab-Israeli war had left the world fed up with Israel. The Ukrainian statesman had gained reputation as a great peacemaker in light of his calming influence during the protests that led to the breakup of Ukraine. Volodymyr's Jewish roots also made him the perfect fit to deal with Netanyahu. The world was demanding a peace treaty, and he was the only one on the planet who could make that happen.

If the UfM would admit Ukraine as an additional member of the ten geographic regions, Antonio Volodymyr would guarantee that the rest of the Eastern Partnership states would support the peace treaty, and deliver Israel on a silver platter.

The tenth antichrist was an amazing fellow.

SEARCH CRITERIA USED IN IDENTIFYING ESAU

1. Seed (lineage/bloodline)

Mixed Jewish-Gentile blood from the <u>house (or a dwelling place) of Esau.</u>

In Hebrew, beth means "house," or "from the house of," or "those who claim to be from a biblical place or name". Houses are mentioned in the Bible for both salvation and destruction.

The phrase 'house of Esau' (Edomites) is mentioned in only one verse of the Bible. In Obadiah 1:18, the Bible says, " *'The* **house** *of Jacob shall be a fire, and the* **house** *of Joseph a flame; but the* **house** *of Esau shall be stubble; they shall kindle them and devour them, and no survivor shall remain of the* **house** *of Esau,' for the Lord has spoken."* (Emphasis added)

Luke 19:9, *"Jesus said to him, 'Today salvation has come to this* **house***, because this man* [Zacchaeus, tax collector]*, too, is a son of Abraham' ".* (Emphasis added)

Esau's descendants are meant for destruction in the last days just before the return of Jesus Christ. Isaiah 63:1–3: *"Who is this who comes from* **Edom***, With dyed garments from Bozrah, This One who is glorious in His apparel, Traveling in the greatness of*

His strength?—"I who speak in righteousness, mighty to save."
Why is Your apparel red, And Your garments like one who treads
in the winepress?" (Emphasis added)

2. *Edom* is Hebrew for "red."

The Bible associates war, sin, and Satan with the color red.
"Red" in Hebrew is *Edom*.

"And the first came out **red**. He was like a hairy garment all
over; so they called his name Esau" (Gen. 25:25, emphasis added).

"Though your sins are like **scarlet**, they shall be as white as
snow; though they are **red** as crimson, they shall be like wool"
(Isa. 1:18, emphasis added).

"Another horse, fiery **red**, went out. And it was granted to the
one who sat on it to take peace from the earth, and that people
should kill one another" (Rev. 6:4, emphasis added).

"And another sign appeared in heaven: behold, a great, fiery
red dragon having seven heads and ten horns, and seven diadems
on his heads" (Rev. 12:3, emphasis added).

"And I saw a woman sitting on a **scarlet** beast which was full
of names of blasphemy, having seven heads and ten horns" (Rev.
17:3, emphasis added).

The universal color of communism from the handbook of Karl
(Mordecai) Marx, who was Jewish, is *red*.

The Nazi swastika is black on a white circle set in a *red*
background.

3. Hatred: self-loathing of Jewish blood

Covenant breaker

Arch-enemy of God

"And the uncircumcised male child, who is not circumcised in the flesh of his foreskin, that person shall be cut off from his people; he has broken My covenant" (Gen. 17: 14).

4. Solution: extreme brutality, no mercy

The desire to more than just shed Jewish blood; desire to wipe the slate clean of the memory of an entire race of people. They have said, *"Come, and let us cut them off from being a nation, that the name of Israel may be remembered no more"* (Ps. 83:4).

5. *"For the life of all flesh is its blood"* (Lev. 17:14).

Jacob, the bloodline of Christ

Esau, the bloodline of antichrist

"Dear children, this is the last hour; and as you have heard that the antichrist is coming, even now many antichrists have come. This is how we know it is the last hour" (1 John 2:18–19).

Addendum II

The world is entering a period of remarkable prophetic years:

- 2014–15—four blood moons are projected to occur on four successive Levitical feast days.
- 2015—*shemittah* year (seventh year) promises rest and abundance, while neglect means judgment.
- 2015–16—marks the 120th jubilee year on the Jewish calendar commemorating Joshua's entrance to the Promised Land in 1414 BC.
- 2017–18—Jewish year 5777 (seventieth anniversary of Israel's rebirth in 1948).

None of these signs are meant to enable us to set definite dates for unfulfilled prophesied events, but as a "watchman" (Ezek. 33:1–6), I am compelled to be a witness.

Most Bible prophecy teachers will tell you that the rapture of the church is the next event on the prophetic calendar. Since Jesus told us that *"no man knows the day or the hour"* (Mark 13:32) of it, I will make no attempt to guess.

But when the church is taken home, as the apostle Paul described in 1 Thessalonians 4:16–28, the man of sin, or Antichrist, will not be far off.

NASA

NASA has calculated that four blood moons and a solar eclipse will take place between April 2014 and September 2015.

Bible students must take guard not to embellish the meaning of blood moons occurring on Jewish holidays. After all, Passover and Sukkot were originally scheduled by God to occur on lunar cycles and are always six months apart.

Yet four blood moons in a row, separated by a lunar eclipse, are noteworthy. The last three times that happened, there were significant events affecting Israel and the Jewish people.

Blood Moons

The first blood moon is forecast during Passover, April 15–22, 2014, the date commemorating the Jewish holiday of the exodus of the Jews out of Egypt.

The second blood moon is predicted to appear during Sukkot, or Feast of Tabernacles, October 8–15, 2014, which memorializes the forty years that the Jews wandered in the desert and lived in temporary shelters, or booths.

NASA has also projected a solar eclipse to occur on March 20, 2015, followed by two more blood moons in 2015: one during Passover, the other during Sukkot.

In the past five hundred years, four successive blood moons have occurred three times:

1492: The Edict of Expulsion began in Spain. King Ferdinand and Queen Isabella gave the Jews fourteen days to convert to Christianity or leave Spain forever. Four successive blood moons occurred in 1493–94.

1948: In fulfillment of Isaiah 66:7–8, Israel was reborn in one day. Four successive blood moons occurred in 1949–50.

1967: In the Six-Day War, Israel preempted an attack from Egypt, Jordan, and Syria. Israel captured the West Bank, East Jerusalem, the Gaza Strip, the Golan Heights, and the Sinai. Israel was reunited for the first time since AD 70. Four successive blood moons occurred in 1967–68.

In 500 BC, the prophet Joel foretold in 2:30–31 that God would use heavenly phenomena before the day of the LORD. His description was later repeated by:

- The apostle Peter in Acts 2:19–20: *"The sun shall be turned into darkness, and the moon into blood, before the coming of the great and awesome day of the LORD."*
- The apostle John in Revelation 6:12–14 (the sixth seal): *"There was a great earthquake; and the sun became black as sackcloth of hair, and the moon became like blood."*

The day of the LORD represents the seven-year tribulation period during which God will deal in wrath and in judgment of those who rejected Christ, and also the time for the final deliverance, blessing, and redemption of Israel. The church, having been previously removed from the earth in what Christians call the rapture, will go to the place that Jesus said He would prepare for them in John 14:3, the New Jerusalem.

For Christians, Passover represents the day that Christ, the spotless Passover Lamb, was crucified as atonement for the sin of the world. Sukkot symbolizes the gathering of God's children to Himself that takes place upon the second coming of Jesus to tabernacle with His people for a thousand years.

2016—70th Jubilee Year

The year 2016 also has special prophetic significance in that it will be a jubilee year on the Jewish calendar. Jubilee years occur every fifty years and hold special significance as the year at the end of seven cycles of shemittah (sabbatical) years. According to biblical regulations, shemittah years had an important impact on the ownership and management of the land of Israel.

Once again, Bible students must take caution since the counting of jubilee years ceased after the destruction of the temple in AD 70. Calculations of the next jubilee year vary with different rabbinical teachers.

The Number 7

The number 7 represents the combination of the divine number 3 and the world number 4. It is used more frequently than any other number in Scripture. Seven is the complete number of God.

There are 7 days in the divine week of Creation: six days of creation (work) and one day for creating (instituting) the Sabbath.

Enoch was the seventh from Adam. Job had seven sons. There were seven days of grace after Noah entered the ark.

Under Old Testament law, an animal must be at least seven days old before it can be sacrificed. A male child could not be circumcised until seven full days had passed.

Jacob served seven years for Rachel. There were seven years of plenty and seven years of famine in Egypt. The land of Israel was to rest in the seventh year. The LORD declared seven feasts. The Feast of Unleavened Bread lasts seven days.

The Savior spoke seven times from the cross.

The number seven is used 52 times in the book of Revelation. The book addresses the seven churches of Asia Minor. There are seven stars representing seven angels who represent seven churches. Jesus is identified as having the seven spirits of God. There are seven seals, seven thunders, seven bowls, and seven trumpet judgments of the tribulation period. The tribulation will last seven years.

The Number 70

Seventy nations make up the descendants of Noah through Shem, Ham, and Japheth in Genesis 10, which provides the genealogy of the nations known at that time.

Seventy people accompanied Jacob on his journey to Egypt (Gen. 46:26–27).

Seventy sevens (490 years) were determined for Israel to complete its transgression and bring in the first coming of Messiah (Dan. 9:24).

"Our days may come to seventy years, or eighty, if our strength endures; yet the best of them are but trouble and sorrow, for they quickly pass, and we fly away" (Ps. 90:10).

The seventy-year anniversary of Israel's rebirth will occur in 2017, the Jewish year 5777.

In AD 70, two blood moons happened at the time of the destruction of the temple.

(God's prophetic calendar, 360 days = 1 year)

✝ ✝ ✝

ENDNOTES

All of the following internet citation were available as of March 18, 2014.

1. http://abcnews.go.com/Health/video-shows-twins-fighting-womb/story?id=17848740#.UcNGgubD_IU
2. http://sacred-texts.com/jud/loj/loj107.htm
3. http://sacred-texts.com/jud/loj/loj108.htm
4. http://themessianicmessage.com/esau_effect.pdf (Esau the Man, Part 1)
5. http://sacred-texts.com/jud/loj/loj108.htm
6. http://jewishencyclopedia.com/articles/4391-circumcision
7. http://philologos.org/__eb-lotj/vol2/onea.htm
8. http://jewishvirtuallibrary.org/jsource/judaica/ejud_0002_0004_0_04318.html
9. http://jewishvirtuallibrary.org/jsource/History/refugees.html
10. Churchill, Winston. *Great Contemporaries*. GP Putnam Sons, Inc. 1937, New York, NY: p. 225.
11. http://philologos.org/__eb-lotj/vol1/six1.htm#1
12. Ibid.
13. http://omegaletter.com/articles/articles.asp?ArticleID=6001 (Obadiah's Indictment)
14. http://wnd.com/2012/06/chariots-in-red-sea-irrefutable-evidence
15. http://sacred-texts.com/jud/loj/loj303.htm
16. http://bible.ca/archeology/bible-archeology-exodus-amalekites.htm
17. http://en.wikipedia.org/wiki/Amalek#Nazis_as_Amalekites
18. JimmyDeYoung,http://prophecytoday.com/news/archive/2006_03_24_archive.php
19. http://jewishencyclopedia.com/articles/11259-nabataeans
20. John Walvoord/Roy B Zook. *The Bible Knowledge Commentary, Old Testament*. David C. Cook Publisher, 1985, Colorado: pg. 654-655.
21. http://jewishencyclopedia.com/articles/4012-captivity
22. http://ccel.org/ccel/josephus/complete.ii.xiv.ix.html
23. http://sacred-texts.com/bib/cmt/clarke/isa034.htm
24. http://ccel.org/ccel/henry/mhc4.Is.xxxv.html
25. http://omegaletter.com/articles/articles.asp?ArticleID=6001
26. http://sacred-texts.com/jud/loj/loj108.htm
27. http://newworldencyclopedia.org/p/index.php?title=Haman_(Bible)&oldid=865163
28. http://en.wikipedia.org/wiki/Julius_Streicher

29. http://sacred-texts.com/jud/josephus/war-1.htm
30. http://sacred-texts.com/jud/t01/t0110.htm
31. http://internationalstandardbible.com/N/negeb.html
32. http://gutenberg.org/files/2848/2848-h/2848-h.htm#link122HCH0008
33. http://sacred-texts.com/jud/josephus/ant-12.htm
34. http://gutenberg.org/files/2848/2848-h/2848-h.htm#link152H_4_0001
35. http://gutenberg.org/files/2850/2850-h/2850-h.htm
36. http://aish.com/jl/h/cc/48942446.html
37. http://gracethrufaith.com/topical-studies/holidays-and-holy-days/the-christmas-story-part-2-conclusion
38. http://home.comcast.net/~rmaurno/Migdal_Eder.pdf
39. http://themessianicmessage.com/esau_effect.pdf
40. http://penelope.uchicago.edu/Thayer/E/Roman/Texts/Tacitus/Annals/15B*.html
41. http://penelope.uchicago.edu/~grout/encyclopaedia_romana/gladiators/nero.html
42. http://penelope.uchicago.edu/Thayer/E/Roman/Texts/Suetonius/12Caesars/Nero*.html
43. http://penelope.uchicago.edu/~grout/encyclopaedia_romana/gladiators/nero.html
44. Ibid.
45. http://gracethrufaith.com/ask-a-bible-teacher/was-nero-the-anti-christ/
46. http://christiantimelines.com/peter_and_paul.htm
47. http://bible.org/article/josephusE28099-writings-and-their-relation-new-testament#P39_9434
48. http://telegraph.co.uk/history/world-war-two/7961211/Hitler-had-Jewish-and-African-roots-DNA-tests-show.html
49. http://historylearningsite.co.uk/austria_and_1938.htm
50. http://law2.umkc.edu/faculty/projects/ftrials/nuremberg/nurembergfrank.html
51. http://www.ess.uwe.ac.uk/documents/osssection4pt1.htm
52. http://history1900s.about.com/od/hitleradolf/a/hitlerancestry.htm
53. http://www.holocaustresearchproject.org/ar/frank.html
54. Brigitte Hamann, *Hitler's Vienna: A Dictator's Apprenticeship*. Oxford University Press, 1999.
55. Ibid.
56. http://www.nizkor.org/hweb/people/h/hitler-adolf/oss-papers/text/oss-profile-04-01.html
57. http://en.wikipedia.org/wiki/Alois_Hitler
58. http://catholicexchange.com/was-hitler-catholic
59. http://jewishvirtuallibrary.org/jsource/Holocaust/hitler.html

60. Ibid.

61. Ibid.

62. http://jewishfederations.org/page.aspx?id=121275

63. http://jewishvirtuallibrary.org/jsource/History/refugees.html

64. http://www.jewishfederations.org/page.aspx?id=47015

65. http://jewishvirtuallibrary.org/jsource/History/refugees.html

66. http://nationalreview.com/articles/212881/father-modern-terrorism/ andrew-c-mccarthy

67. http://tomgrossmedia.com/ArafatArticles.html

68. http://jpost.com/Middle-East/Egypt-grants-citizenship-to-50000-Palestinians

69. http://www.rbooker.com/old-site-files/html/the_myth_of_yasser_arafat.html

70. http://jewishvirtuallibrary.org/jsource/biography/arafat.html

71. http://www.nationalreview.com/media-blog/34973/egyptian-magazine-confirms-arafat-was-behind-munich-olympic-and-other-murders/tom-g

72. Ibid.

73. http://nationalreview.com/articles/212881/father-modern-terrorism/ andrew-c-mccarthy

74. Ibid.

75. http://jewishvirtuallibrary.org/jsource/Terrorism/achille.html

76. http://jewishvirtuallibrary.org/jsource/Peace/madrid1.html

77. http://prophecytracker.org/2011/05/the-abrahamic-covenant-unfolds-2/

78. http://mfa.gov.il/MFA/ForeignPolicy/MFADocuments/Yearbook7/ Pages/419%20Statement%20by%20Yasser%20Arafat-%2014%20 December%201988.aspx

79. http://avalon.law.yale.edu/21st_century/roadmap_hearings.pdf

80. http://www.cfr.org/israel/oslo-ii-accords-interim-agreement-west-bank-gaza-strip/p9676

81. http://www.wnd.com/2000/10/6491/

82. http://bbc.com/news/world-middle-east-25205170

83. http://www.haaretz.com/print-edition/news/arafat-s-doctor-his-blood-had-hiv-but-poison-killed-him-1.227311

84. http://bbc.com/news/world-middle-east-25205170

85. Sada, Georges. *Saddam's Secrets*. Thomas Nelson, Inc. 2006, Nashville, TN: pp. 70-71

86. http://visionandvalues.org/2007/09/anti-semite-saddam-outdid-ahmadinejad/

87. http://nytimes.com/2011/02/06/world/middleeast/06iraq.html?_r=1&

88. http://history1900s.about.com/od/saddamhussein/a/husseincrimes.htm

89. http://defense.gov/home/dodupdate/For-the-record/documents/11152005.html

90. Sada, Georges. *Saddam's Secrets*. Thomas Nelson, Inc. Nashville, TN: pp. 252-254

CPSIA information can be obtained at www.ICGtesting.com
Printed in the USA
LVOW13s0723070714

393081LV00003B/120/P